About Time

The Frontiers of Theory

Series Editor: Martin McQuillan

About Time

Narrative, Fiction and the Philosophy of Time

Mark Currie

Edinburgh University Press

Edinburgh University Press Ltd
22 George Square, Edinburgh

Typeset in Adobe Sabon
by Servis Filmsetting Ltd, Manchester, and
printed and bound in Great Britain by
CPI Antony Rowe, Eastbourne

Transferred to digital print 2008

A CIP record for this book is available from the British Library

ISBN 978 0 7486 2424 9 (hardback)

Contents

Series Editor's Preface

Since its inception Theory has been concerned with its own limits, ends and after-life. It would be an illusion to imagine that the academy is no longer resistant to Theory but a significant consensus has been established and it can be said that Theory has now entered the mainstream of the humanities. Reaction against Theory is now a minority view and new generations of scholars have grown up with Theory. This leaves so-called Theory in an interesting position which its own procedures of auto-critique need to consider: what is the nature of this mainstream Theory and what is the relation of Theory to philosophy and the other disciplines which inform it? What is the history of its construction and what processes of amnesia and the repression of difference have taken place to establish this thing called Theory? Is Theory still the site of a more-than-critical affirmation of a negotiation with thought, which thinks thought's own limits?

'Theory' is a name that traps by an aberrant nomial effect the transformative critique which seeks to reinscribe the conditions of thought in an inaugural founding gesture that is without ground or precedent: as a 'name', a word and a concept, Theory arrests or misprises such thinking. To imagine the frontiers of Theory is not to dismiss or to abandon Theory (on the contrary one must always insist on the it-is-necessary of Theory even if one has given up belief in theories of all kinds). Rather, this series is concerned with the presentation of work which challenges complacency and continues the transformative work of critical thinking. It seeks to offer the very best of contemporary theoretical practice in the humanities, work which continues to push ever further the frontiers of what is accepted, including the name of Theory. In particular, it is interested in that work which involves the necessary endeavour of crossing disciplinary frontiers without dissolving the specificity of disciplines. Published by Edinburgh University Press, in the city of Enlightenment, this series promotes a certain closeness to that spirit: the continued exercise of critical thought as an attitude of enquiry which counters modes of closed or conservative opinion. In this respect the series aims to make thinking think at the frontiers of theory.

Martin McQuillan

Acknowledgements

I would like to thank many of my friends and colleagues who have taken an interest in this book, talked me through its issues, invited me to present its material in states of unreadiness, and urged me towards its completion. I am very grateful to Anna Snaith, Becky Beasley, Markman Ellis, Rachel Potter, Peter de Bolla, Nick Royle, Peter Barry, Patricia Waugh, Peter Nicholls, Sean Matthews and Drew Milne for their input and support. I am filled with gratitude and respect for my colleagues at Anglia Ruskin University between 2000 and 2005, and would particularly like to thank Rick Rylance, Rebecca Stott, Nora Crook, Rick Allen, Nigel Wheale, Peter Cattermole, Simon Featherstone, Ed Esche, John Gilroy, Ted Holt, David Booy, Mary Joannou, Catherine Silverstone, Gianna Bouchard, John Gardner, Katie Price, Sue Wilson, Vicky Williamson, Eugene Giddens, Alex Byrne, Sally Cline, Pauline Dodgson-Katiyo, Vernon Trafford and Rowlie Wymer for everything they did to support me and the project. I would like to thank Jackie Jones and Martin McQuillan for their very efficient and positive response at each stage of the project's development, and Sarah Hall for many important editorial contributions.
There was a single first-year lecture that I used to give at the University of Dundee called 'Story Time' which was about the idea of novels which were about time. It focused on the relationship between time as a theme and what I called the temporal logic of storytelling in Kurt Vonnegut's *Slaughterhouse Five*. In the eight years that I delivered that lecture, it developed into a polemic against thematic approaches to time in fiction, and argued that fictional narratives had much more profound effects on our relation to time than could be achieved by merely addressing time as a topic. Some of this argument survived into a course I taught at Anglia Ruskin University in Cambridge between 2000 and 2005, called 'Narrative in Culture', which focused on novels about time in relation to ideas about time in philosophy and cultural theory. The students of 'Narrative in Culture', and various other

modules at Anglia Ruskin were enormously influential on the content of this discussion, and I would particularly like to mention Edna Johnston, George Selmer and Sarah Thwaites. There is no doubt that my earliest interests in time were produced by my clever parents, and by my brother and sister, and taken forward later by many fantastic and ridiculous conversations with Nick Gardiner and Duff Donaldson on the subject of the existence of time. Rob and Jane Young made an indirect but enormous contribution in the form of their generous support throughout 2005. The most important person has been Tory Young, whose intelligence as a reader I can only recommend to the rest of the world.

To Tory

Chapter 1

Introduction: About About Time

My title both chastises me for the tardiness and congratulates me for the timeliness of my book. In 1989, David Wood predicted that 'our century-long "linguistic turn" will be followed by a spiralling return to time as the focus and horizon of all our thought and experience' (David Wood 2001: xxxv), and it is about time that this prediction about time came true. The need as I see it is partly as Wood described it: the need for a 'programme for the analysis of temporal structures and representations of time' (xxxvi). Alongside such a programme, there is also a need for a theoretical account of time which might rescue the analysis of temporal structures from some of the vagueness of new historicism, cultural history, Derridean hauntology, the uncanny and the cultural theory of postmodernism. It is particularly in relation to fiction, to the strange temporal structures that have developed in the novel in recent decades, that a clear framework for the analysis of time seems necessary. But there is also a need to revisit the relation of fiction and philosophy because of these strange temporal structures, to ask what domain of understanding or knowledge might be occupied by the contemporary novel on the subject of time, or what effects these structures might exert in the world.

The word *about* has turned out to have a resonance for my topic that I didn't fully anticipate. If primarily it means 'on the subject of', it carries within it a set of general problems about the content of language and, for my purposes, a specific question about fiction: what does it mean to say that a fictional narrative is 'on the subject of' time? Many who have written on this topic have chosen to focus on novels which are manifestly, perhaps intentionally, about time. Commonly this involves detailed readings of novels which are addressed unmistakably to the question of time at the level of theme and content. It is also reasonably common to find a less content-based, more formalist sense of 'about', according to which experimental narrative forms and techniques are seen to place time at the forefront of a novel's thematic concerns. Such novels are about time in the sense that they explore the theme of time, perhaps even the nature of time, through the temporal logic of storytelling.

Paul Ricoeur is one of those who believe that some fictional narratives are about time and others are not. He proposes, in Part 3 of *Time and Narrative*, that it is possible to distinguish between *tales of time* and *tales about time*. All fictional narratives, he claims, are tales of time 'inasmuch as the structural transformations that affect the situations and characters take time'. Tales about time, on the other hand, are those in which 'it is the very experience of time that is at stake in these structural transformations' (101). Time is a universal feature of narrative, but it is the topic of only a few.

This boundary between the 'of' and the 'about' will be difficult to establish.[1] For Ricoeur, the distinction is fundamental for the so-called *Zeitroman*, but his attempts to establish it are riddled with tautology and contradiction. First he selects the most cooperative and incontrovertible examples of the *Zeitroman* – Woolf's *Mrs Dalloway*, Mann's *The Magic Mountain* and Proust's *In Search of Lost Time* – and takes as his analytical project the staggeringly circular goal of demonstrating that these are indeed tales about time. The interest in this section of *Time and Narrative* lies in the difficulty Ricoeur encounters in this apparently self-affirming project. 'That *The Magic Mountain* is a novel about time is too obvious for me to have to insist upon the fact' but it is 'more difficult to say in what sense it is one' (1985: 112). Three pages later, *The Magic Mountain* is 'therefore not simply a tale about time' but one which presents a 'problem': 'how the same novel can be both a novel about time *and* a novel about a deadly sickness' (115). This worsens as the 'destiny of European culture becomes what is principally at stake' (116) and the *Zeitroman* becomes subordinated within the framework of a *Bildungsroman*. This problem of what is 'principally at stake' in a novel becomes something of a refrain in Ricoeur's discussion, proving the 'aboutness' of the premise with the 'at stakeness' of the discovery. *Mrs Dalloway* is about time because the conflict between internal duration and the exteriority of clock time is 'ultimately at stake', just as Proust's novel is a quest in which 'what is at stake is, precisely, the dimension of time'. As in *The Magic Mountain*, *In Search of Lost Time* can only be about time if time is what is at stake, so that it cannot be claimed, as Deleuze has done that 'what is principally at stake . . . is not time but truth' (1985: 131).

The problem of *aboutness* will never be far away in the discussion that follows, and for the moment I would like to make two observations about it. The first is that in Ricoeur's account of the 'tale about time', it is not necessary that time be the only topic, but rather that it predominates. It must be what is principally, but not exclusively at stake. As a critical stance, this is strikingly similar to the question of form and structure in narrative as it was approached in Russian formalism and structuralism in the mid-twentieth century. There, the proposition in question was not that all fictional narratives are about time, but that they were, variously, about form, about structure, about language or about narrative itself. Fredric Jameson describes structuralism, for example, as 'a kind of transformation of form into content, in which the form of structuralist research . . . turns into a proposition about content: literary works are about language' (1972: 198–9). If we look at Jakobson's method of dealing with this problem, we see that it resembles Ricoeur's resort to the idea of predominance. For Jakobson (1960) there were six functions of language which co-existed in any given utterance, but only when one of the functions predominated could the utterance be said to be 'about' that function. The second observation I would like to make about the question of the tale about time follows from the first – from the familiarity of the problem to the structuralist. Jakobson is perhaps not typical of structuralism in the sense that he is happy to view the form of an utterance itself as the topic of some discourses. Many would claim that the content of every discourse was its form. For the structuralist, there was a danger in saying that some works were about form and others were not. We might, for example, adopt the classical position that poetry somehow orientated its message towards form more than prose did, in the sense that it highlighted the formal structure of its medium. Prose on the other hand aimed at a kind of transparency – it aimed exactly to disguise the formal aspects of its communication in the dream of transparent reference to the world. The characteristic response to this in structuralism was that the highlighting of formal properties in poetry and the disguise of these properties in prose does nothing to suggest that form is somehow more centrally a feature of the former than the latter. In fact the danger is that we will fail to notice the formal properties of the most transparent discourses, confusing linguistic with phenomenal reality. It is therefore more important to consider the most transparent discourses to be about form than those that openly declare themselves to be so, because the role of unmasking is necessary in the former case and unnecessary for the latter. It is this sort of argument that underlies Barthes's position on the 'unhealthy signifier' which effaces its own status as a linguistic sign, or on the realistic novel which aims to hide the structurality of its structure.

This argument can be quickly illustrated in relation to the novel. We might reason that Sterne's *Tristram Shandy* is a novel about the form of fictional narrative because it comically highlights formal conventions in the novel. The corollary of this sense of 'aboutness' is that we might view a novel such as Jane Austen's *Emma* as a transparent depiction of the world. In *Tristram Shandy*, the form of the novel itself could be said to be what is principally at stake in the narrative, whereas in *Emma*, what is principally at stake is matrimony and social mobility. For the structuralist, such a claim was bogus precisely because the novel which disguises its textuality is no less textual than the one which declares it. More generally, language which denies that it is language is no less linguistic for it, just as the denial that one is bourgeois does not make someone less bourgeois, and may even make them more so. In this situation, the critic must focus efforts on the unmasking of those tales normally considered not to be about form, about structure or about language, since it is those discourses which are wearing masks, or involved in any kind of deceit. To say that language is a universal feature of all discourses but the topic of only a few is to allow the deceit to stand. If we translate the terms of this discussion into the question of time, of the tale about time, we find a basis for the claim that all novels should be viewed as tales about time. If time experiment in the novel is an exploration of the theme of time, or the nature of time, through the temporal logic of storytelling, it is only so because the temporal logic is unconventional. If we say that a narrative which obeys a more conventional temporal logic is not about time, we are merely succumbing to its naturalisation. When we think that narratives are not about time, we are accepting the way that conventional narrative temporality has embedded a certain view of time in our universe.

This is one of the positions that this book aims to explore – that it is important to see all novels as novels about time, and perhaps most important in the case of novels for which time does not seem to be what is principally at stake. Ricoeur's stance on this issue seems unnecessarily bossy, and depends on the authority of the interpreter in the act of identifying what is principally at stake. This kind of authority is in evidence in the everyday interpretation of semiotic objects as much as in the academic study of art and literature, and particularly when the true subject of an artwork is a matter for debate, but in academic contexts, no more than in cinemas or art galleries, these are debates conducted without a rational foundation of the kind that can only be provided by a theoretical account of the concept of 'about'.

The second major area of resonance of the word 'about' for my study is derived from its long career in crossword clues, and carries the hidden sense of 'backwards', of turning about and running in the opposite direction. 'About time' is backwards time, and the idea of a backwards temporality at work in narrative is the major emphasis that this project brings to the study of narrative temporality. Narratives are often not only *about time*, but they are *about about time*, that is, on the subject of the backwards motion of time.

Imagine reading a novel with a bookmark. Suppose the novel is read from the beginning to the end, in the right order and for the first time. The bookmark will move over time from the beginning to the end of the novel and as it does, it will represent the reader's present in the narrative. Everything to the left of it is in the past, already known, and everything to the right of it is in the future, and not yet known. The past of the narrative is fixed in a way that the future of the narrative is not. Anything could happen. At first glance, this reflects the way that time works in life. We inhabit the present, which is sandwiched between a fixed past and an open future. But there are some obvious differences. The present for a reader in a fictional narrative is not really the present at all but the past. It is somebody else's present related to us in the past tense. Though it seems like the present, because it is new to us, it is tensed as the past, in what the French call the preterite, a tense otherwise known as the past perfect or the past historic. We are narrated to in the preterite, but we experience the past tense in the present. But because it is the past tense we know that there is a future present, in relation to which the present of the narrative is past. Peter Brooks points out that there is a tradition of narrative criticism, including Vladimir Propp, Jean-Paul Sartre and Frank Kermode, which views the act of telling a story as fundamentally different from life because 'in telling everything is transformed by the structuring presence of the end to come, and another, opposite tradition, including Claude Bremond and Jean Pouillon, for whom the action of a novel takes place before the eyes as a 'kind of present' (1984: 22). The relation of this quasi-present of reading to the structural retrospect of tense in the novel is an issue to which this book returns in each of the chapters that follow. A fictional narrative encourages us to think of the past as present no more than it encourages us to think of the present as a future past. But whereas narrative theory has explored the first implication, of what Ricoeur calls the presentifying[2] of the past, exhaustively, through the themes of memory, the reliability of the narrator and other aspects of retrospect, it has paid far less attention to the correlative issue in which the present is experienced in a mode of anticipation.

Narrative is understood as retrospection more readily than it is understood as anticipation, but it cannot really be one without also being the other. If, in order to look back at what has happened, we tell a story, we must also know that the present is a story yet to be told. The present is the object of a future memory, and we live it as such, in anticipation of the story we will tell later, envisaging the present as past. The present might be lived in anticipation of some future present from which it is narrated, but this may also entail the anticipation of events between the present present and the future present from which it is narrated which will also be part of that story. For many years, the study of narrative has been attending to the notion of the present as a place from which we continuously revise stories about the past, and much less attentive to the relationship between storytelling and the mode of continuous anticipation in which we attach significance to present moments. There are some excellent studies of fiction in relation to the philosophy of time, but the approach is usually orientated around the search for lost time, around the remembrance of things past and the way they inhabit the present. The concern of this book is with the relationship between storytelling, future time, and the nature of being. It begins from two propositions. The first is that the reading of fictional narratives is a kind of preparation for and repetition of the continuous anticipation that takes place in non-fictional life. The second is that the place of fictional narrative in the world has altered since the beginning of the twentieth century, and that fiction has been one of the places in which a new experience of time has been rehearsed, developed and expressed. These propositions give fiction, and the study of fiction, a critical role in the understanding of what lies outside of fiction.

This question of anticipation, or of a mode of being which experiences the present as the object of a future memory, has one of its fictional correlatives in the structural retrospect of the novel, but it can also be related to the question of prolepsis, or the kind of fictional flashforward that conjoins a 'present' moment to a future one. The idea that this anticipatory mode of being might be a characteristic of contemporary culture, the contemporary novel, and even of human being in general is one that informs the discussion of the first three chapters of this book. Chapter 2 looks at the concept of the present from Augustine's puzzle about the non-existence of the present to Derrida's critique of the metaphysics of presence. The aim of this chapter is to consider the contemporary novel in the context of social theories of time and philosophical accounts of time. It takes three concepts of time in contemporary cultural theory, which it names as time–space compression, accelerated recontextualisation and archive fever, and three philosophical approaches to time which have some relevance for a future-orientated theory of narrative and which are derived from Husserl, Heidegger and Derrida. In the context of these ideas, the chapter argues against the predominance of 'retrospective' models of narrative, such as Linda Hutcheon's 'historiographical metafiction', as a basis for characterising the contemporary novel. Chapter 3 offers an analytical framework for the concept of prolepsis designed to take the term forward from Genette's influential account in such a way that it is capable of accounting for effects formerly considered as metafictional. Chapter 4 turns back to philosophy in order to establish a set of connections between temporality and self-consciousness. Like the idea of retrospect in narrative theory, the idea of self-consciousness has played a significant part in critical characterisation of the contemporary novel, and this chapter aims to show the inseparability of a problematic of self-consciousness from the philosophy of time. Chapter 5 follows these issues into the question of inner and outer time, and turns attention on the Augustinian foundations of modern philosophies of time, and an analysis of the narrative aspects of Augustine's *Confessions*. Chapters 6 and 7 pose a question about the nature of knowledge in fiction, and the difference between what a novel knows about time and what a philosopher knows. These chapters involve readings of Graham Swift's *Waterland*, Martin Amis's *Time's Arrow*, Ali Smith's *The Accidental*, and Ian McEwan's *Saturday*. Finally, Chapter 8 explores the potential impact of tense philosophy on narratology and asks the question of whether it is possible to infer a metaphysics of time from the linguistic form of narrative. In each section of this discussion there is an attempt to bring about a useful conversation between the temporality of narrative and the philosophy of time.

Notes

1. The potential confusion of 'tales of time' and 'tales about time' is illustrated by Genevieve Lloyd, who begins her otherwise very accurate exposition of Ricoeur by getting this the wrong way around: 'But not all novels are "tales of time"' (Lloyd 1993: 12).
2. Ricoeur is following both Schiller and Gunther Muller here. See *Time and Narrative*, Part 3, p. 66 for the former and p. 78 for the latter. But the terms are also used in Heidegger and Husserl in various forms.

Chapter 2

The Present

The present, as philosophy knows well, doesn't exist, and yet it is the only thing which exists. The past has been, and so is not, and the future is to be, and so is not yet. That only leaves the present. But as long as the present has duration, any duration at all, it can be divided into the bits of it that have been, and so are not, and the bits of it that are to be, and so are not yet, so that the very duration of its existence consigns it to non-existence. The problem here is obvious: the relationship between presence and existence is logically circular, or tautological in the manner of a claim that a = a. Worse than that, the tautology is embedded in the tense structure of language, which insists that 'has been' and 'will be' are equivalent to 'is not', since what 'is' must be rendered in the present. The claim that what 'has been' 'is not' barely constitutes a claim at all, since all it does is to relive the conspiracy of being and presence which inhabits tense.

The complicity of presence and being, and its incumbent logical problems, hangs over all notions of the present, so that the analytical framework of tense acquires a metaphysical importance. In this discussion, three notions of the present are in question: the historical present, the philosophical present and the literary historical present. In relation to the first, I intend to invoke a set of ideas about a new experience of the present which is produced by social and technological change, ideas which have been used to characterise the contemporary world. Second, there is the idea of presence, the understanding of presence as it has been approached in philosophy, and particularly the ways in which it has been complicated and rejected in philosophy after Heidegger and Husserl. Finally, there is the question of the 'contemporary novel', what that means, and how it participates in and analyses this changed experience and understanding of time. In each case then, for the world, for philosophy, and for the novel, the notion of the present is divided between the thing reflected upon and the apparent modernity of the reflection.

Social Theories of the Present

The notion that the present, understood as the contemporary world, or the historical present, is marked, or even characterised, by a changed experience of the present can be approached in a number of ways. I would like to offer three ways into this discussion, under the following headings: (1) Time–space compression; (2) Accelerated Recontextualisation; and (3) Archive Fever. To begin with, we might look to David Harvey and Fredric Jameson, both of whom have developed versions of the claim that the experience of the present has somehow changed. Harvey, for example, in his discussion of time–space compression (1989: 240–59) begins from the position that the time taken to traverse space, whether at the infinite speed of telecommunications or the relative speed of jet travel, produces a compression of time horizons 'to the point that the present is all there is' (240). Harvey traces this process as a change in the way that space and time are represented: a gradual process of representing the whole of the earth within a single spatial frame, from Renaissance mapping to the first photographs of the globe from space. Time–space compression of this kind has implications for the experience of the present partly because it extends the span of the present to encompass places once thought to be at a considerable spatial, and therefore temporal, distance. The telephone, like the view of earth from space, creates a co-presence or simultaneity between Europe and Australia which has greatly expanded the temporal and spatial horizons of the ordinary conceptions of the present and presence. In Jameson's analyses, there is a similar emphasis on the expansion of the present as a kind of underlying logic in the contemporary phase of multinational capitalism. Our contemporary social system, Jameson claims, has begun to 'lose its capacity to retain its own past, has begun to live in a perpetual present and in a perpetual change that obliterates traditions of the kind which all earlier social formations have had in one way or another to preserve' (1992: 179). Something of Lacan's account of schizophrenia is at work in this characterization, in the sense that there is some loss of temporal order, of the linear admission of meanings which organises a discourse, or a sentence, in time. The sense of orderly significance in which meanings are spread out in time has therefore yielded to a chaotic co-presence of meanings, as if all the words of a discourse constitute a kind of babble produced by their simultaneity. The very thought of global simultaneity which Harvey regards as the characteristic frame of the modern mind evokes this babble, in the form of a multifarious totality suspended in an ineluctable present. If 'presence' is divided between spatial and temporal properties, between the spatiality of 'here' and the temporality of 'now', these supposedly new experiences of the present seem to offer an account of its contamination by the 'there' and the 'then', or the spatiotemporally absent.

Many of the most compelling theories of the contemporary advance some version of this contaminated present, and some account of the collapse of temporal distance into simultaneity. Accounts of postmodernity were generally preoccupied with the difficulty, if not impossibility, of continuous novelty, innovation or originality, and therefore often characterised postmodern originality as mere repetition, recycling and recontextualising of past forms. The notion of postmodern style as 'accelerated recontextualisation', or the recycling of the increasingly recent past, is one model on which the present is understood as the bearer of historical traces. 'Recontextualisation' can of course mean many things: an everyday object is recontextualised when it is placed in an art gallery, and a Shakespeare play is recontextualised when it is read in relation to the war in Iraq. In cultural criticism and the advertising industry, however, the term commonly indicates some kind of reference to the styles of the past: some revival of a previous aesthetic through the repetition of its forms and fashions. To take clothing design as an example, it is clear that the fashion of the 1990s and since was proceeding in a linear sequence through the decades of the mid-twentieth century, recontextualising styles from the 1960s before moving on to the 1970s and 1980s. It might look at first as if the recontextualisation of clothing style must observe a respectable gap between the original and its recontextualisation. Wearing a kipper tie in 1982, after all, would simply be deemed unfashionable, whereas by 1990 it had acquired the ironic weight of a recontextualisation, and similarly the resurgence of the flared trouser leg had to respect a period of absence which marked the gap between the original style of the 1960s and 1970s and its repetition in the 1990s. The point about accelerated recontextualisation, however, is that this gap becomes increasingly, if not infinitely, short, so that the temporal distance between an original and its recontextualisation is abolished altogether. If the irony of the kipper tie depends on temporal distance, the acceleration of the cycle of recontextulisation in general must dispense with the ironic content of recontextualisation in general, so that the repetition of past aesthetic styles becomes value-free. The style of the present, according to the logic of accelerated recontextualisation, is more obviously constituted by traces of the past, which are no longer held at a distance by the temporal gap between the present and the past. This is perhaps most apparent in technological areas of commerce such as music, television or computing, in which the speed of recycling is unrestrained, so that, for example, the television advertisement can produce parodic representations of films which are on current release, or popular music can refer to current events. It might be claimed that fashion, and perhaps design in general, alters the present by reaching into the future as much as it reaches into the past. Design, as a form of in-built obsolescence, ensures the renewal of markets for its product in the future. It may be that there are aspects of design which still link the notion of the present, or of modernity, to the idea of progress: that technology in the present is better than it used to be, and worse than it will become. But in most areas of contemporary commerce, the notion of progress is, at best, an alibi, and more often the notion of newness is better understood as a self-serving value, with no function other than to connote newness itself. If clothing styles remained the same, frozen by edict, the notion of the contemporary, of the present, would be liberated from its frantic commercial pace, and no longer marked by its imminent and immanent obsolescence. As an aesthetic commodity, the present anticipates its own pastness in its very form, and is experienced, like everything else in the contemporary world as the object of a future memory. In the mode of accelerated recontextualisation, the process which consigns the present to memory is conducted at infinite speed, since the present commodity is always already in the past.

This commercial logic, the so-called acceleration of social time, opens into the idea of archive fever: the frenzied archiving and recording of contemporary social life which transforms the present into the past by anticipating its memory. The temporal structure of a present lived as if it were the object of a future memory is the primary focus of this book, and the central tenet of its theory of narrative. But it is clearly also a characteristic of what is thought of as contemporary society by those in the most commercial and media driven economies. Archive fever, as it is described by Derrida, is above all a future orientation, or a mode of anticipation, which structures the present:

> . . . the archive as printing, writing, prosthesis, or hypomnesic technique in general is not only the place for stocking and for conserving an archivable content *of the past* which would exist in any case, such as, without the archive, one still believes it was or will have been. No, the technical structure of the *archiving* archive also determines the structure of the *archivable* content even in its very coming into existence and in its relationship to the future. The archivization produces as much as it records the event. This is also our political experience of the so-called news media. (1996: 17)

Archivisation is our experience of the so-called news media because the cause-and-effect sequence of an event and its recording as news is reversed in a highly developed media capitalist society: an event is recorded not because it happens, but it happens because it is recorded.

We know this from many decades of photography, and now, in an accelerated way, from the digital video camera: the present which is recorded is produced by the possibility of photography, by the act of photographing, and would not take place otherwise. The archive is not a passive record, but an active producer of the present: an 'archiving archive' which structures the present in anticipation of its recollection. We know this also from narrative consciousness, which is by no means an exclusive characteristic of the contemporary world, but which is now assisted by a technological army of recording and archiving devices. Narrative is the ancient, as well as the contemporary, version of this consciousness, which lives its experience as if it were recorded in the preterite tense, and conceives of its future actions as things that will make good stories, and good memories. The structure of the archiving archive, or the envisaged future which produces the present as memory, is the heart of narrative. The only claim that might be made for archive fever in relation to contemporary society, therefore, is that it is an accelerated, and technologically assisted, version of a phenomenon as inherent in the human condition as the telling of stories. Nevertheless, the grip that this fever currently has on the world of personal and collective self-representation is not to be underestimated or ignored on the grounds that it has a history.

The Vanishing and Banishing of the Present

These three notions of the contemporary – time–space compression, accelerated recontextualisation and archive fever – which are rooted in the idea of a transformed concept and experience of the present, are certainly not alien, or even new, to philosophy in its dealings with the concept of presence. In fact, an exploration of the philosophical analysis of presence raises some difficulties which challenge the basic vocabulary of the sociological accounts offered above: difficulties which relate to issues such as the *concept* and the *experience* of the present. To designate some relevant philosophical inquiries into these aspects of the present, I would like to gloss three well-known notions which characterise approaches to the present in phenomenology and its critique: the present as a crossed structure of retentions and protentions, anticipatory resoluteness, and the logic of supplementarity. The first heading refers to Husserl's account of the present, the second to Heidegger's emphasis on future-orientation as the foundation of *being*, and the third to Derrida's critique of temporal hierarchy in philosophical thinking. Under each heading I intend to offer only the most basic account of a trajectory of philosophical thought on the present and presence, and taken together, a kind of philosophical context for the observations which follow on questions of the present and presence as they occur in the contemporary novel. It is also worth observing, at the outset, that the three former headings, which sketch some new experience of the present, offer not only an account of time-consciousness, but of some degree or mode of self-consciousness, whether personal or collective. The compressed global stage, the intense now-awareness of recontextualisation, and the self-distance involved in archive fever are all conditions in which a subject is self-consciously aware of its representation, or its perception from the outside, from the point of view of another. The conjunction of time and self-consciousness is a constant one in philosophy, but less so in approaches to the contemporary novel, and this in one of the areas in which narrative theory can benefit from an engagement with philosophical approaches to the present.

In Husserl and Heidegger, there is a reworking of Augustine's notion of the vanishing present. For Augustine, the present lacks extension: in its undivided form, the present is infinitely small, or without duration, and if it is given extension, in the form of some block of time to be designated as presence, that presence will be necessarily divided between elements which have been and those which are still to come. The present is therefore never before us, and any designated duration, whether it be a lifetime, a year, a month, a day, the duration of a song, or of a note in a song, it is subject to this logic of division, and therefore condemned to vanish. The elusiveness of 'now' becomes, for Augustine, the elusiveness of time in general, since in the vanishing of 'now', time loses its foundational concept. Hence in the celebrated example in *Confessions*, Augustine compares the passage of time to the recitation of a psalm, in which the text of the psalm passes from the future into the past, and the now of this recitation is comprised only of the awareness or memory of that which has already been and the expectation of that which is still to come. Husserl begins his essay *The Phenomenology of Internal Time-Consciousness* with more or less the same analogy: that of a melody in which the now is understood as the sounds which are still present to consciousness, and concludes that this presence is structured by retentions and protentions, or elements of the past which are retained in the consciousness and those which are present as anticipatory expectation. This simple observation – that presence is never present – is a fundamental and recurring tenet in the work of Heidegger and Derrida, both of whom contrast an ordinary conception of time, based on the uncritical conception of time as a sequence of *nows* with one in which presence is divided. For Heidegger and Derrida, there is much more at stake than a set of debates in metaphysics. The vanishing now of Augustine's ruminations on time create severe difficulties for the very idea of being, since being and presence are so subtly entwined in our thinking, and entwined also with the idea of linguistic meaning. The starting-point in this chapter was that the idea of existence was somehow tautologically inherent in tense structure, or perhaps more accurately the temporal reference of linguistic structures, and this point can be easily extended from the notion of existence to those of being, reality and indeed to most problems in the philosophy of language. In the work of both Heidegger and Derrida, then, there is a rejection of presence and the present as an undivided, or self-identical foundation for time, or indeed for anything which exists in time, which is everything. And whereas in Augustine and Husserl there is a preoccupation with memory and retention (which in Husserl are related but not identical facets of consciousness), in Heidegger and Derrida there is an emphasis on future-orientation: on that aspect of the present which projects forwards in anticipation or expectation of things to come. It is in this framework that Heidegger's *anticipatory resoluteness* and Derrida's *logic of supplementarity* can be most readily understood. Anticipatory resoluteness is a mode of being associated by Heidegger with authenticity (a topic which receives more detailed treatment in Chapter 4), entailing a mental activity of projection forwards to death which is inherent in human being. This mode of anticipation is a way in which the envisaged future marks the present, structures the present, so that the very being for which presence is supposed to act as a foundation is structured by the non-being which it anticipates. There is a sense here in which something in the future is seen to inhabit the present, and therefore functions in a way which is homologous with the anticipation of retrospect which we discussed as archivisation earlier. In fact, the thinking behind 'archivization' is derived directly from Heidegger's emphasis on the future, and might be schematised as what Derrida refers to as the 'logic of supplementarity' (1973: 89). Again this is a logical scheme which is returned to throughout the chapters of this book, but which requires a preliminary characterisation here. One of the patterns of thought that Derrida, with his Heideggerean background, often fixes upon is the explanation which views the 'supplement' as somehow secondary to the 'origin'. The supplement is to be understood here as something extra which comes afterwards, and which Derrida's readings consistently show have some conceptual priority over the origins from which they are supposed to follow. The logic of supplementarity, for Derrida, is a counter-logic which such explanations carry within themselves. This is to say that an explanation which secures itself on the scheme of an originary presence followed by a supplement which is extra and secondary will often contain its own counter-logic which suggests the supplement is in fact prior. It is this logic of the supplement which underlies the account of archivisation offered above, and which views the envisaged future memory as a causal agent in the present. A phenomenon as widespread as news-consciousness, or as digital video self-archiving, can be said to have its philosophical equivalent in the division of the present, and in the emphasis on the future which characterises Heideggerean anticipation and Derridean supplementarity.

This set of issues about the present and presence follow quite different trajectories outside the tradition of phenomenology. For many thinkers about time the very idea of the present is horribly egocentric and must be banished in the name of objectivity. The present is, after all, a kind of perspectivism which centres any enquiry in the spatial and temporal position of a particular person or set of persons. But what would it be like to think about time without the concept of the present, or to think about anything without the notion of presence. Such an approach is often favoured by theoretical physicists who adopt the 'block universe' view of time in order to eliminate the perspectivism of an account of time organised around the past, the present and the future. It is a logical consequence of the rejection of the present that the dependent notions of the past and future are also banished, since their existence is entirely relative to the present. What is being rejected here is a *tensed* view of time, and what is being adopted is an *untensed* view of time. Understood at its most basic level, tense is a relation between the time of an utterance and the time of the event being spoken about. The position from which I began this discussion, namely that the present is the only thing which exists, and yet also does not exist, is not foisted upon us by the tensed view of time. There are, of course, philosophical positions which consider the past to have existence of a kind which is not accorded to the future, so that the past and the present are deemed to exist, or have reality, while the future exists in an open state, as possibility which passes into actuality. Such a view does some justice to the direction of time and represents a widely held assumption that the future is ontologically distinct from the present and the past. Untensed views of time, however, generally hold that there is no ontological distinction between the past, present and future, and that in order to purge understanding of its egocentricity and its linguistic aberrations, time must be viewed as a single dimension. The untensed view of time therefore maintains that the future exists, and that the ontological priority of the present is an error produced by the mere psychological experience of time.

The remainder of this chapter applies some of these social and philosophical approaches to time to an understanding of narrative, and more specifically to an understanding of the nature of contemporary fiction. It aims in particular to explore the role of a tense framework in the characterisation of contemporary fiction.

Narrative Fiction and the Present

One of the obvious things that can be said about a fictional narrative is that, in the relationship between a text and its reading it offers a kind of model of time. The reading of a novel, for example, like Augustine's recitation of a psalm and Husserl's description of listening to a melody, involves the passage of events from a world of future possibilities into the actuality of the reader's present, and onwards into the reader's memory. Read in the right order, therefore, the novel is asymmetrical in the same way that time is, since the present of the reading becomes a kind of gateway through which words, descriptions and events pass in their transition from the realm of possibility into the realm of actuality. The experience of reading, thus described, corresponds to a tensed conception of time and represents the egocentric, or subjective, pole in the relation of the reading subject to the textual object. The untensed view of this relation would therefore correspond to the text itself, to its determinate number of pages, verbal structures and sequence of events from beginning to end. A text, as an object, corresponds to a 'block universe' account of time, and therefore to the notion of time cleansed of unwanted egocentricity, of the psychological clutter of a given reading, and as such represents the pole of objectivity. As far as the subject/object relation goes, the reading of a novel offers a more sophisticated model than the stock philosophical examples of tables, trees in the wood, or Oxford college quads, partly because of the temporality of reading. The most basic reflections on this analogy between reading and living, however, throw up some of the fundamental problems in the philosophy of time. It would seem sensible, for example, to view the relation of tensed and untensed approaches to time as being as inseparable as the relation between subject and object. The idea of tensed and untensed conceptions of time as polemic opponents looks deficient from a philosophical point of view, just as it is deficient to think of a text and its reading as somehow incompatible with each other. Phenomenological approaches to the act of reading have referred to the reading process as one of actualisation or concretisation to reflect this coming-into-existence of the events of a narrative as they pass from the future into the present and the past, and therefore offers a model of time in which the tensed and the untensed views of time exist in a dynamic relation with each other. It is useful here to think of the terminology associated with the tradition of Anglo-American philosophical approaches to time, which distinguish between tensed and untensed approaches to time as the difference between the A-series and the B-series. The A-series represents a view of a sequence in terms of the past, the present and the future, while the B-series represents the time of a sequence as a block, in which the relations between events are understood as a sequence of times and dates in which events relate to each other in terms of *before* and *after*. In the A-series, or in A-theory, the present seems to have a special ontological status which brings with it a set of questions about the reality of the past and the future, while in the B-series, or in B-theory, the sequence of time is a kind of spatialised block in which all events are seen as existing together. The debates between these positions, and accounts of their interaction are complex, and are the subject of more extended discussion in Chapter 8. But for our present purposes it is worth considering the application of the A-series and the B-series to the understanding of a narrative fiction. An A-theory of narrative fiction would involve attention to the moving present of the reader, while the B-theory would view the narrative as a block in which the sequence of events should be understood as having before and after relations. We find an A-theory narratology, for example, in the analysis of point of view in the sense that it takes account of the control and distribution of information in fiction, and attends to questions of what a reader does and does not know at particular stages of a reading. We find a B-theory narratology at work in literary structuralism, for example, when it views the temporal sequence of a narrative as a structure. The emphasis on opposition in structuralist narratology, for example, tends towards B-theory because it looks at temporally separated components of a narrative as if they were co-present, perhaps viewing the beginning and ending of a novel in terms of co-present poles, or the contrast of good and bad characters as structural oppositions. Of course, in real acts of narratological analysis it is almost impossible to prevent the A-series of a narrative from merging into its B-series, the tensed sequence of reading from interacting with the untensed, objective sequence of the text, and this in itself demonstrates the difficulty of a separation of a sequence of time as an object from the egocentric experience of that sequence. Would it in fact be possible to talk about a novel entirely as a B-series without regard for the linear sequence of nows which would comprise the egocentric experience of a reading? And reciprocally, would it be possible to talk about the tensed present of reading without reference to the relations of before and after of the linguistic sequence of a text, or of the imagined temporal sequence of narrated events? It is one of the achievements of narratology to organise the many different time loci involved in reading, and in the interaction between a reader and a narrative text, into some kind of analytical framework, and it might also be considered one of the great achievements of narrative fiction that it can act as a kind of warning to philosophy against the simplicities of distinctions such as that between the tensed and the untensed conceptions of time.

In the relation between fiction and life, however, there is an important ontological boundary which is normally understood as the difference between being and non-being. If we think about this in terms of the idea that a narrative fiction provides a model of time, and that this model consists primarily of the interaction between the tensed and the untensed conceptions of time, there is an obvious and interesting problem. Put simply the problem is this: in life the future does not exist yet, but in narrative fiction, it does. Of course there are many problems with such a proposition, one of them being the idea that something fictional can exist, or perhaps more accurately, it could be said that the only reason that the future can exist in fiction is that things in fiction don't exist. Theoretical physicists, fatalists and other B-theorists may disagree from the other point of view, that in life, the future does exist just as it exists in fiction, but that, imprisoned as we are in the ineluctable present, we have no access to it. These objections are not really obstacles to the argument about time and narrative that I want to present, because both recognise a certain difference of access to the future between the fictional and the real universe. Whether this ontological boundary is redrawn, blurred or erased, the world of narrative is one in which the future has already taken place, and is not open. According to this perspective, the tensed view of time, in which only the present exists, and the block view of time, in which the past and future are equally existent, interact because in the act of reading we are experiencing the past as quasi-present, and not because there is any ontological difference between fiction and life. The relevant ontological category here is *written text*, rather than *narrative* or *fiction*. In the oral delivery of a story, the future is open, and particularly so if I am making it up as I go along. In written text, the future lies there to the right, awaiting its actualisation by the reading, so that written text can be said to offer a block view of time which is never offered to us in lived experience. But this is as true for fictional narrative as it is for non-fictional narrative, since the existence of the future is clearly produced by the structure of temporal reference in a written narrative, and not by the nature of fiction itself.

If the written narrative offers a model of time, then, it offers one which is fundamentally at odds with what we might call 'lived experience'.

There is, as J. R. Lucas expresses it, a fundamental modal difference between the past and present on one hand and the future on the other:

> The future is not already there, waiting, like the reel of a film in a cinema, to be shown: it is, in part, open to our endeavours, and capable of being fashioned by our efforts into achievements, which are our own and of which we may be proud. (1989: 8)

The unreality of the future, its openness, contrasts with the already-there-ness of the future on the reel of a film, and by extension with the already-there-ness of the future in writing, whether it is a novel, an autobiography, a history, a psalm or a melody. We might ask why Augustine and Husserl don't attend to this modal difference more explicitly when they use the psalm or the melody as a model of time, or view the fictional narrative, considered as a model of time, as flawed by this already-there-ness of the future. The answer to this question, however, goes some way towards the identification of a key philosophical issue which has generally been absent from the discussion of time in narrative, and which also helps to locate the key concerns in the future of this discussion. In Lucas's discussion there is a clear conviction that thought can do no justice to the passage of time and the direction of time unless it upholds this distinction between the reel of a film and the lived experience of time. But this is not to say that the mind is not capable of some temporal tourism:

> Although in point of fact we are necessarily located in the present, in our imagination and thought we are free to adopt any temporal standpoint, past, present or future, that we please, and view events thence. It is a deep metaphysical fact that though in our bodies we are time-bound, in our thoughts we are not. I, my mouth, my body, my hand, am imprisoned in the twentieth century. But my mind is free to range over all time. (1989: 11)

The philosophical problem here, which has some place in narrative theory, is fairly simple. The tradition of thinking about time which runs from Augustine to Husserl is one in which Augustine's theistic conception of untensed eternity gives way to an entirely tensed phenomenology of internal time-consciousness. In Husserl's account of the melody, as in subsequent phenomenological accounts of reading, the past, the present and the future exist strictly as a unity in human consciousness. In Lucas's view, which I am using to represent a broadly Anglo-American philosophical approach to the question of the future, the mind is free to roam in time, but the body is stuck. This separation of the body and the mind, and by extension, of time and temporality, is exactly what is not admissible in phenomenology, which restricts itself to the study of phenomena as they are apprehended in human consciousness, and so can admit to no mind-independent view of time, or to anything other than imprisonment in the mind. How then does this difference between the time of the mind and the time of the universe affect the idea of narrative as a model of time? In Lucas's view, the mind is free to roam, but this is imagination and not reality. According to this view, the reel of a film, or the sequence of words in a book, are reifications of the mind's freedom to adopt any temporal standpoint, to imagine and to roam, but because it is mere imagination, it follows that the reel of a film or a fictional narrative cannot provide a reliable model of time. If we take the already-there-ness of the future as the touchstone for this unreliability, or of the difference between written narrative and life, it becomes necessary to identify two distinct problems: that of retrospect and that of fictionality. In the case of retrospect, the already-there-ness of the future is a product of temporal reference, whether the future is imagined or actual, and in the case of fictionality, the already-there-ness of the future is the product of the mind's freedom to invent the future. The difficulty of distinguishing between these kinds of textual future might be attributed to the conventions of narrative which borrow the future's already-there-ness of non-fictional retrospect for the purposes of authenticating the future's already-there-ness in fiction. In the effort to separate the mind from reality, and therefore render the fictional narrative useless as a model of time, it would appear that the ontological objection that the future exists in fiction but not in life is implicated in a more general problematic, namely the temporal reference of retrospect.

Where does this leave the idea that narrative is fundamentally different from life? It is clear in the argument above that the existence of the future in narrative depends somewhat on the idea of writing or recording. It might be more reasonable to claim that it is writing in general which fails to correspond with the nature of time by virtue of its determined and accessible future, and therefore that if we think about narrative, as much recent narrative theory is inclined to do, in more general terms, the problem evaporates. If, for example, we think of narrative not as writing but as a mode of consciousness, or perhaps, with Derrida, think of writing in a massively expanded sense as something which encompasses experience more generally, we go some way towards resolving the asymmetry between narrative and time. Similarly, we might regard the existence of the future in written narrative as irrelevant on the grounds that, like future events more generally, this existence is actualised only by the passage of events from possibility to actuality in the act of becoming present. The as yet unread future of a narrative, it might be argued, is no different from the future in general in the sense that the reading of future words and events has not yet happened, and therefore does not exist. These two ideas, of narrative as a kind of consciousness rather than as a kind of writing, and of the non-existence of the future of written events are positions from which it might be possible to rescue the idea of narrative as an inadequate model of time. The second counter-argument, however, that the future of a text and future moments in general are, ontologically, on a par is not immediately convincing, and here we uncover what is really meant by the idea that a narrative is a 'model of time'. The idea of an ontological difference between the exist-ence of the future in text and the existence of the future in general sur-vives this objection fairly easily, since it is the ability of a reader to take an excursion into the future, to jump ahead and return to the present, that has no obvious analogy in lived experience. What is more, the unknowability of the future in a block universe is largely predicated on the collective nature of the present, and again there is no correlative for this in the fictional narrative as a model of time. Many people may be reading the same book as me, but the present of these readings will all differ from each other, so that some will finish, and so know the future, before others. It is the collective imprisonment in the same present that gives the notion of objective or cosmological time its meaning, and this ineluctability of the collective present can not be reflected in the reading of a written narrative. It is more rational to think of the narrative, the already-there-ness of its future, and its tangible block view of its own uni-verse, as a model which exactly fails to represent the ontological condi-tions of human being. In this failure, the model of time which is offered by narrative does its work by crossing the boundary between actual and potential futures to produce a hermeneutic circle between narrative and time, which encourages us to envisage futures on the model of teleo-logical retrospect which narrative encodes.

One of the striking abilities of the fictional narrative, as Genette has analysed, is its freedom to roam in time, and particularly in the use of the anachronies of analepsis and prolepsis. The discussion in this chapter began by pointing to a distinctively modern temporality which experi-ences the present as the object of a future memory. The full discussion of prolepsis, and the interaction between fictional prolepsis, which involves an excursion into an 'actual' future, and non-fictional prolepsis, which involves an excursion into a potential future, is the subject of the discus-sion in Chapter 2. By way of preparation, however, it is worth noting that there is something performative about this relationship, in the sense that a discursive utterance has the power to bring a state of affairs into being. This is by no means the whole story of the performative, as the next chapter will argue, but it may be fruitful to contemplate the enormous increase in the use of prolepsis in fiction, film and television of the last three decades. It is perhaps part of the more general self-knowingness of these narrative media that they should seize upon the already-there-ness of the future in the verbal structure of fiction, or, as it used to be, the 'reel' of the film, and bring it to the forefront of narrative experimentation. It is not my intention to focus on filmic versions of proleptic narratives, but it is clear that there is an increasing preoccupation with the proleptic plot that runs from Nicholas Roeg's *Bad Timing* to the generation of films that follow from Tarantino's *Pulp Fiction*. In contemporary fiction, the flashforward has become established as a fundamental device not only of the self-conscious experiments of metafiction, but as a realist mode of storytelling. There is no easy formula with which to encapsulate the relation of narrative prolepsis and the philosophical problem of the relation of time and narrative, but we might start by observing that prolepsis flaunts the kind of freedom to roam that we associated earlier with the mind, the imagination and fiction. We might also view this as a symptom of divided presence: that is, as a version of that modern experience of time which tends to install within the present traces of the past and future. Prolepsis can be regarded as a kind of instruction in the significance of events in the light of later events or outcomes, and this is the very definition of teleological retrospect. It is too easy to view the anachronistic tendencies of contemporary narrative fiction either as some introverted self-analysis on the part of the novel on the conventions of narrative, or as some mere passive imitation of a new experience of time which is external to the novel, and at work in social reality. The assumption in this discussion, however, will be that the ascendance of anachrony, and in particular the fashion for prolepsis, is a performative function which produces in the world a generalised future orientation such that the understanding of the present becomes increasingly focused on the question of what it will come to mean.

The Novel's Now and the Novel Now

The Derridean problematic of presence brings Augustine's puzzle of the vanishing present, Husserl's account of the present as a crossed structure of protentions and retentions, and Heidegger's priority for the future in being-towards-death, to bear on the structure of the sign. In Derrida's essay, 'Differance' (1982: 1–27), for example, the division of presence is the basis of the trace structure of the sign, which is to say that the concept of the sign is no more the container of meaning than the present is the container of presence. If we think of the sign, we might say that it bears within it retentions of the past which are of various sorts. The sign depends upon former uses which have established its meaning by convention, and cannot signify in the present without these retentions of the past. Perhaps more importantly, the sign is embedded not only in a history, but in a linguistic chain, a sequence of words which provide the discursive context for its meaning. It would be impossible to argue that the sign, understood as the word, in some way carries its meaning around with it, and deploys it in the same way in any context. The sequence of words in a sentence, for example, ensure that any word is marked by those other words which precede it and follow from it in the sequence. If we think about the moving *now* of the sentence, it is clear that a sophisticated combination of the tensed and the untensed views of time are at work in its production of meaning. There might be some kind of controlled admission of words as they pass from the sentence's future into its past, but there must also be a view of the sentence as a whole, or of some larger unit of discourse which comes into view as a block, and of which the *now* of reading is a survey. In Derrida's argument, this means that the common idea of a word as somehow a container of meaning is no more intelligible than the idea of the present without the concepts of the past and the future. Traditionally, linguistics has viewed the word as a carrier of meaning in the sense that it can operate on its own, out of context, or in different contexts, as a minimum free form. The phoneme on the other hand means nothing in itself, and only comes to signify in combination with other phonemes when they combine to make larger blocks such as words. But this view of significance is subject to the same laws as Augustine's vanishing present, in the sense that there is no limit to the division of presence involved in the model of significance as a sequence of nows. If phonemes have duration, they can be divided, and similarly it can be argued that words must retain and await the past and future of a sequence in a way that is comparable with phonemes. But the problem of distinguishing between the word and the phoneme in terms of sequence-dependence does not simply banish the notion of the present or of the presence of meaning. A sentence, for example, requires the controlled, linear admission of meanings, as well as the block view. If the words of a sentence were encountered simultaneously rather than in order, they would obviously fail in their mission to signify, and a reader incapable of viewing a sentence as a dialectic of tensed and untensed views of time would be unable to read.

There is as yet no poststructuralist narratology which has responded to the problems of presence at the level of the narrative sequence. There are three distinct ways in which this presents an opportunity or a problem for narrative theory. First, there is the need for narratology to analyse the *now* of narrative sequences in terms of a dialectic between the tensed and untensed approaches to discursive time. Second, there is the question of the extent to which the divided presence of the *narrative now* has become an issue in the contemporary novel itself, that is to say, the extent to which the novel has come to understand itself as the discourse in which the trace-structure of moments can be most adequately explored. To this problem we might attach the claim that there is in contemporary fiction a prevalence of the analeptic and proleptic excursion, which enacts the trace-structure of moments in the refusal of linearity, as well as the claim that prolepsis has come to dominate over analepsis among the interests that narrative fiction has taken in its own temporal logic. In prolepsis, narrative can reflect and produce the future orientation that has been outlined here in relation to Heidegger's Being-towards-death and Derrida's *différance*. The third issue follows from the second, and the claim that prolepsis, or future orientation in general, might in some way characterise the contemporary novel. The issue for narrative theory here is a literary-historical one, but it concerns also the most multifarious and complex conceptions of the present to which literary criticism might devote its attention, namely the literary-historical present itself. The remainder of this chapter will concern itself with the latter of these problems.

The notion of the literary epoch has received considerable critical attention in recent decades, but these attentions have not often been focused on the notion of the contemporary. The discussion above indicates some basic problems for the notion of the contemporary novel, of the role that it may have to play in the production of modern temporal experience, for what it might have to contribute to discussions about time, but also for what it means to talk of the contemporary at all. If contemporary means 'happening now', it is subject to the same problems of duration and existence as the notion of 'now' more generally, and this is going to be a particular problem for the phrase 'contemporary fiction'. There are many senses in which contemporary fiction cannot be understood as happening now, and I do not intend to explore the many paths that open up here into deliberate misunderstandings of that phrase. The most common usages are probably those of the university module which calls itself 'contemporary fiction', where the phrase often designates fiction from the Second World War onwards, and those of the non-academic fiction-reading world for whom the contemporary is much closer at hand. In both cases, the set of referents is enormous, and in both cases there is a necessary reduction of a multiplicity which operates through a kind of hegemonic struggle as a result of which particular novels come to represent their age. In the world of academic literary studies this is no different from the canonical nature of reading lists in earlier periods, where canons are understood as forms of domination always open to revision by some new form of domination. If we take Kermode's phrase 'forms of attention' (Kermode 1985) as the currency which assigns value to these hegemonic works, it is plausible to view the newspaper-based fiction industry as an elaborate mechanism which bestows attention on particular works in a manner analogous to that of the academic process, but in a more commercial context. Nor would we want to claim that these two worlds are entirely, or even at all, separate. The sociology of academic value-judgements is not my primary interest, but I take it as a basic truth that the works of contemporary fiction which attract forms of attention, be it money or academic discussion, acquire their hegemonic position, as concrete universals, as a result of forces which cannot be reduced to arbitrations of quality. What does interest me is the way in which works might satisfy the conditions of representative-ness, that is, the way in which some fictional writing might be assumed to possess the characteristics of their epoch, and the extent to which this assumption is transposed into value, understood as a cluster of aesthetic value, exchange value and durability. The relationship between the char-acteristics of a novel and the idea of the present as an historical totality is one of the factors which will determine the contemporaneity of con-temporary fiction, as if the very idea of the contemporary contained within it a double reference, on one hand indicating mere present-ness, and on the other the special power to represent the present. An example of this circular relation between ideas of the present and ideas of the con-temporaneity of contemporary fiction can be found in Linda Hutcheon's influential formulation in *A Poetics of Postmodernism* (1988) that so-called 'Historiographic Metafiction', in which the metafictional concerns of the Modernist novel converge with issues in historiography to produce a kind of fiction which is uniquely capable of fulfilling the 'poetics of post-modernism'. If in the study of the Modernist period the hypercanonicity of Joyce and Woolf deprive a large sector of fictional production in the period of attention, so that the epoch is represented through a few deviant experiments, it is doubtless because of a complimentary force which rep-resents the age in terms of a movement inwards, with Nietzsche, Freud and phenomenology, and which is corroborated by the techniques of nar-rative introversion, stream of consciousness and indirect discourse. For Hutcheon, the postmodern age is dominated by certain unresolved con-tradictions between history and fiction, arising from a generalised dis-trust of official facts, and a blurring of the boundary between events and facts as represented. The postmodern novel, then, is represented as one in which metafictional concerns are followed into questions about the representation of the past, and novels which are not of this kind do not represent their epoch. Yet the contemporary world that one might construct from the historiographic metafiction would be a hopelessly partial portrait, not least because the present world is not present in historiographic metafiction. If we think of novels such as John Fowles's *The French Lieutenant's Woman* and *A Maggot*, J. M. Coetzee's *Foe*, Salman Rushdie's *Midnight's Children*, Graham Swift's *Waterland*, Julian Barnes's *Flaubert's Parrot* and *A History of the World in 10½ Chapters*, Umberto Eco's *The Name of the Rose*, William Golding's *Rites of Passage*, Peter Ackroyd's *The Great Fire of London*, A. S. Byatt's *Possession*, John Updike's *Memories of the Ford Administration*, Robert Coover's *The Public Burning* or Pat Barker's *Regeneration*, it is apparent that an interest in the fictional representation of history does indeed underlie a significant strand of contemporary fiction. Nevertheless, Hutcheon's argument that the historiographic metafiction is the paradigmatic postmodern novel has produced a distorting account of the fictional epoch, not only because there are countless novels which show no concern for the paradoxes of fictional and historical representation. The partiality of such a picture is inevitable. But where Hutcheon promotes the idea of representative-ness in the form of a circle between a kind of novel and a contemporary world concerned with 'issues surrounding the nature of identity and subjectivity; the question of reference and representation; the intertextual nature of the past; and the ideological implications of writing about history' (1988: 117), she goes some way towards effacing the agency of the academic literary critic in the construction of this circle. If the novel has developed preoccupations with the representation of history, of the status of facts and the textuality of history, it has done so in the same period in which academic literary studies has witnessed a resurgence of historicism, reanimated exactly by questions of identity, subjectivity, reference and representation, intertextuality and ideology. The representative-ness of the historiographic metafiction is a straightforward hegemonic representation of the interests of a particular social group as universal values, and that social group is represented most fully by the academic new historicist. If the novel's now has some analogical relation to the idea of the present moment, the novel now has a similar relation to the contemporary world in general at a higher level of complexity. The four issues involved in this problem – the present of reading, the present moment, the contemporary novel and the contemporary world – are customarily stabilised through the imposition of some kind of structure of exclusion which will stipulate the limits of the present's duration or the parts which will represent the totality. The counter-manoeuvre being offered here is to displace these structures of exclusion with a kind of analysis committed to the future orientation which, as it has been suggested, characterise the present moment, the now of reading, the contemporary novel and the collective experience of time which characterises the modern world.

What then does it mean to say that the contemporary novel might be characterised by future orientation? One possible answer to this question is taken up in the next chapter, which aims to analyse the prevalence of prolepsis in contemporary fiction within a wider framework of a culture increasingly conscious of its own present as the object of a future memory. Part of the purpose of the next chapter is to show that even the apparent preoccupation with retrospect in historiographic metafiction can be understood as a kind of future orientation, and particularly when temporality is understood in terms of the formal structure of narrative in general. One of the striking tendencies in critical writing about fiction in the twentieth century is what might be called its thematicisation. One way to illustrate this tendency is to think of the relationship between fiction, criticism and theory as it existed in the formalist period and the way that this relationship is transformed in a period concerned with the historical content of literary works. In literary structuralism, for example, theory designated a body of work in linguistics which provided a descriptive framework for the analysis of literary form. In the case of literary narratology, this meant establishing a set of codes and conventions in relation to which narrative meaning was generated. For the structuralist narratologist, the question of what a fictional narrative was about was one which was bracketed, or made secondary to questions about how they signified through a set of internal and external relations. Theory, in this context, means something akin to 'analytical framework', and, as its critics were quick to point out, in this sense 'theory' was quite alien to the nature and content of fiction. Increasingly, however, theory has come to designate a set of ideas about the nature of language, culture, history and identity, ideas which are then identified as the actual content of fiction. Linda Hutcheon's work is an example of this tendency to understand theory as a kind of fictional content:

> Historiographic metafiction shows fiction to be historically conditioned and history to be discursively structured, and in the process manages to broaden the debate about the ideological implications of the Foucaldian conjunction of power and knowledge – for readers as for history itself as a discipline. As the narrator of Rushdie's *Shame* puts it:
>
>> History is natural selection. Mutant versions of the past struggle for dominance; new species of fact arise, and old, saurian truths go to the wall, blindfolded and smoking last cigarettes. Only the mutations of the strong survive. The weak, the anonymous, the defeated, leave marks . . . History

loves only those who dominate her; it is a relationship of mutual enslavement.

(1983, 124)

The question of *whose* history survives is one that obsesses postmodern novels like Timothy Findley's *Famous Last Words*. In problematizing almost everything the historical novel once took for granted, historiographic metafiction destabilizes received notions of both history and fiction. (1988: 120)

This citation within a citation exemplifies a relation between fiction, criticism and theory from which we need to rescue ourselves. Here the notion of theory is transformed from that of 'analytical framework', from something alien to the nature of content and the nature of fiction, to being the content of fiction itself. Likewise, the role of the critic is reduced to that of identifying theoretical content in fiction, and of passing between theory and fiction in a way that affirms their reciprocity and their mutual support. Gone is the hermeneutics of suspicion, and the notion of critique. By constructing the relation of mutual affirmation between postmodernity and the postmodern novel as historiographic metafiction, the critical act is reduced to something less intellectually engaged than the heresy of paraphrase, and something more like an assemblage of statements which, if paraphrased, might be saying more or less the same thing. This is also the danger of the more general notion that contemporary novels are about time: that the philosophy of time and the novelistic treatment of time might be arranged alongside each other in a pointless demonstration that statements about time in philosophy and fiction might be alike. It is only when a degree of formalism is allowed back into the analysis that the critic can do justice to the nature of narrative: to the fact that its statements about time are inevitably involved with their temporal structure, or that time is a theme of narrative, but it is also part of the temporal logic of storytelling. This means that when it is the explicit content of a narrative, in the way that history is the explicit content of narrative in Rushdie's *Shame* and Findley's *Famous Last Words*, it is least interesting to us. For this reason also, Ricoeur's distinction between tales about time and tales of time might be seen as an attempt to focus the notion of fictional narrative's engagement with time on those novels in which time is a theme. It is in relation to the formal logic of temporal structure, and to the form of internal time-consciousness, and not at the level of theme, that narratology can properly attend to the question of the present, and the ways that it is marked by the future.

Chapter 3

Prolepsis

This chapter is about the anticipation of retrospection and the extended significance that this temporal loop has acquired in our world. I am going to approach the subject through three different meanings of the word *prolepsis*, or, since the primary significance of prolepsis is anticipation, three different types of the anticipation of retrospection. The first of these I will refer to as the *narratological* meaning of prolepsis: a term used by Genette and others to describe flashforward. Prolepsis, for Genette, is a moment in a narrative in which the chronological order of story events is disturbed and the narrator narrates future events out of turn. The narrative takes an excursion into its own future to reveal later events before returning to the present of the tale to proceed with the sequence. As Genette makes clear, this is far less common in narrative fiction than its counterpart, *analepsis*, or flashback, but it will be my contention here that prolepsis is the more rewarding analytical concept. For reasons that will become apparent, I will set aside the second meaning of prolepsis, which will receive a fuller treatment in a moment. The third meaning I will refer to as *rhetorical* prolepsis, to designate a phenomenon well-known to classical orators and scholars of rhetoric: the anticipation of an objection to an argument. This is a technique used to preclude objections by articulating them, and even answering them within an oration, and it will be one of the trajectories of this discussion to analyse the extended scope of this device both in contemporary fiction and the world of discourse more generally. My question for this chapter then is how the rhetorical and the narratological senses of prolepsis can be linked.

The phrase *anticipation of retrospection* refers to a temporal structure which lies at the heart of the human experience of time, as Heidegger taught us,[1] but also at the heart of narrative, both in its mode of fictional storytelling and as a more general mode of making sense of the world. Narrative is generally retrospective in the sense that the teller is looking back on events and relating them in the past tense, but a reader or listener experiences these events for the first time, as quasi-present. Even in a second reading of a novel, it can be argued, the reader decodes the past tense as a kind of present, since it is an aspect of readerly competence to understand what is not yet known. There are many studies of narrative that have emphasised this strange interaction between the temporality of the narrative and that of the reader. Peter Brooks summarises the tension neatly when he observes:

> If the past is to be read as present, it is a curious present that we know to be past in relation to a future we know to be already in place, already in wait for us to reach it. Perhaps we would do best to speak of the *anticipation of retrospection* as our chief tool in making sense of narrative, the master trope of its strange logic. (1984: 23)

I argued in Chapters 1 and 2 that the fictional convention which encourages a reader to view the past as present has as its counterpart the tendency to view the present as past, or as the object of a future memory. In other words the present of a fictional narrative and the lived present outside of fiction are both experienced in a future anterior[2] mode: both are, in a sense, experienced in the preterite tense in relation to a future to come. When we read a novel we make present events that are in the past, and when we live life we often do the opposite: we live the present as if it were already in the past, as if it were the object of a future memory. If in reading a narrative we decode the preterite as a kind of present, the process is one of presentification,[3] whereas in living we use a kind of envisaged preterite to deprive the today of its character as present.[4] Put simply, it is possible that the reading of narrative fiction, in instructing us in the presentification of the past, also robs us of the present in the sense that it encourages us to imagine looking back on it.

Brooks's point is an observation about the tense conditions of fiction, and not about prolepsis itself. It demonstrates that anticipation is structural in that condition insofar as the present of fiction is lived in grammatical acknowledgement of the time of narration, which is a future that is already in place. In life, however, the future time of narration is not already in place in the same way. When we find the preterite encroaching on the lived present in the self-narration of an adventure or the digital recording of visual experience, we project forward to an envisaged time of narration in order to render the present as narrated time. I began this discussion with an intention to connect the devices of narratological and rhetorical prolepsis, but in this basic tense structure of classical narrative fiction we have identified a more pervasive kind of prolepsis, which can be placed between the narratological and the rhetorical as a kind of bridge: the anticipation of retrospection which is involved in all narrative, and which offers the beginnings of a theory which connects the temporality of reading with the temporality of living. This is the second meaning of prolepsis that I set aside in the opening paragraph. The connection that it offers between reading and life can be expressed in the following preliminary proposition: that there is a hermeneutic circle between the presentification of fictional narrative and the depresentification of lived experience.

This proposition will reappear in different guises throughout this book, and I intend to leave the full exposition of the hermeneutic circle of presentification and depresentification for later. To move towards this it is necessary to be more analytical about the relation of this general anticipation of retrospect, which I will call *structural* prolepsis, to *narratological* and *rhetorical* prolepsis. Beginning with fictional narrative, it is possible to identify three time loci which structure the communication: the time locus of the narrated, the time locus of the narrator, and the time locus of the reader. This is a traditional framework which underlies much of the narratological study of fiction. In the work of Muller and Genette, the relationship between the time locus of the narrated and the time locus of the narrator is given special prominence, so that the tension of narrated time and the time of narration has become the predominant temporal framework in the study of fictional time. Ricoeur's analysis of fiction, for example, takes this distinction as its starting point and pursues it through the analysis of time experimentation in the Modernist novel. In the terms of this framework we can classify our three types of prolepsis as follows:

1. Prolepsis 1 is narratological prolepsis, and is a form of anticipation which takes place within the time locus of the narrated. It is the anticipation of, or flashforward to, future events within the universe of narrated events.
2. Prolepsis 2 is structural prolepsis, and is a form of anticipation which takes place between the time locus of the narrated and the time locus of the narrator. It is, among other things, the relation between narrated time and the time of narration which is inherent in the preterite tense of classical narration.
3. Prolepsis 3 is rhetorical prolepsis, and is a form of anticipation which takes place between the time locus of the narrator and the time locus of the reader.[5] The classical form of Prolepsis 3 is the anticipation of an objection and the preclusion of that objection by incorporating a counter-argument into the discourse.

Though I have linked Prolepsis 2 with the hermeneutic circle of presentification in fiction and depresentification in life, it will be the burden of this argument to show that all three forms participate in this hermeneutic circle, though not always operating within the terms of presentification and depresentification. It should also be observed from the start that whereas Prolepsis 2 is a property of all fictional narrative, Prolepsis 1 and 3 are devices which come and go in fiction, and are often viewed as forms of experimentation, or deviation from narrative norms. This difference recalls the discussion in Chapter 1, of Ricoeur's distinction between tales *of* time and tales *about* time, since Prolepsis 2 designates a function inherent in all fiction, while Prolepsis 1 and 3 point to features of fiction which indicate a conscious concern with the temporality of narrative. When the boundaries between these three categories of anticipation are questioned, this distinction between the conscious and the unconscious concern with narrative temporality also comes into question, and it is part of the movement of this discussion to subvert this sense of the *aboutness* of fiction about time.

Prolepses 1, 2 and 3 are so arranged to respect a chronological order: narrated time is anterior to the time of narration which is in turn prior to the time of reading. Prolepsis 1 comes first because its forward projections fall within the time locus of narrated time; Prolepsis 2 is next because it spans narrated time and the time of narration; and Prolepsis 3 is chronologically third because it spans the often enormous gap between the time of narration and the time of reading. As always however, this chronology bears little resemblance to the phenomenological temporality of reading, in which a reader is not simply posterior to the text but also starts at its beginning and is duly sent forward by the projections of Prolepsis 1 and 2, and in the process, will be addressed by Prolepsis 3. Chronologically we have a line, but phenomenologically we have a loop. Though the reader may be located years, centuries or even millennia after the narrated time of a given narrative, Prolepsis 1 will project that reader forward through narrated time to a future which, in chronological terms, is located in the distant past. Or to put it another way, in the act of reading, the reader's present will have embedded in it another present which is the decoded preterite of fictional narrative.

The description of narrative temporality has a tendency, like the description of tense in general, to hurtle towards an absurd complexity. The source of much of this absurdity is the collision of what Ricoeur calls cosmological and phenomenological time, as witnessed in the preceding paragraph. Cosmological time, for Ricoeur, is clock time, objective time, linear time, and is underpinned by the philosophical tradition which views the time line as a succession of 'nows'. Phenomenological time, on the other hand, is something more like the embedding structure referred to in the previous paragraph, in which former presents exist as if embedded inside each other as the constituent parts of a perpetual present. This is one of the problems on which the analytical value of prolepsis hinges. If words such as past, present and future, which are founded in the objective linearity of clock time come into contact with the phenomenological view of time as a structure of embedded presents, the result will be a kind of confusion. The idea of time as succession will be rendered inoperable by the idea of time as co-existence. This is particularly clear in the case of the reading of a narrative. We have already identified three presents involved in the simplest of narrations: the present of narrated time, the present of the time of narration, and the present of the time of reading. While the scheme of Prolepses 1, 2 and 3 organises these chronologically on a time line, the phenomenology of reading threatens to destroy the foundations of prolepsis altogether, drawing the notions of past and future into the present in such a way that the anteriority of the past and the posteriority of the future are questioned. The result is a mishmash of pasts that take place in the future and futures which take place in the past, as the terminology of cosmological time strains to assert itself within the perpetual present of phenomenological time.

In the sections that follow, I will proceed from apparently straightforward instances of prolepsis to enormously complicated ones, and from instances as they occur in fiction to those that operate non-fictionally.

Problems in the Definition of Prolepsis

Prolepsis 1 offers a rudimentary training in the anticipation of retrospect, by jumping ahead within the time locus of narrated events to a future point, which is often an outcome. This creates an effect that is sometime referred to as teleological retrospect,[6] that is, a looking back from an endpoint. To look back on an event is to give it a significance it did not possess at the time of its occurrence. If we think of a time line, we might say that the present is the most advanced, the latest, or the most modern existing point in that line. Though in life we might anticipate events which are posterior to the present, these anticipated events are not yet in existence, and involve the projection forward to an entirely imagined future. This is not the case in narrative fiction, where we might view the future of a narrative as a future which is already in place, one which has a spatial existence in writing, in the form of words which lie to the right of the bookmark, or those words which are not yet read. By making an excursion into a future which is already in place, fiction can therefore instruct us in the kinds of significance acquired by an event when it is looked back upon in a mode of teleological retrospect.

Various modes and levels of Prolepsis 1 operate in fictional narrative. Though we generally know it when we see it, a satisfactory definition is difficult to produce and can uncover interesting problems in the founding assumptions of narrative temporality. The most unproblematic examples are those which take place in narratives which firmly establish a chronological linear sequence, so that a disruption of that pattern is clearly discernible. Muriel Spark begins Chapter 3 of *The Driver's Seat* with the following excursion into the future of the narrative:

> She will be found tomorrow morning dead from multiple stab-wounds, her wrists bound with a silk scarf and her ankles bound with a man's necktie, in the grounds of an empty villa, in a park of the foreign city to which she is travelling on the flight now boarding at Gate 14. (1974: 25)

This narrative about a woman who goes on holiday to be murdered, establishes a simple sequence of events of preparing for, travelling to and reaching an anonymous urban destination, and departs from the chronological sequence at each stage by flashing forwards to the scene of, and sometimes the subsequent newspaper reporting of, her death by murder. In this example, prolepsis is particularly marked because it is rendered in the future tense, and this is because the 'now' of the novel takes place, unusually, in the present tense: 'She stops at the bookstall, looks at her watch and starts looking at the paperback stands' (1974: 21). If the narrative were more conventional in its use of tense ('She stopped at the bookstall'), the prolepsis might be marked by a tense which indicates a future event in relative terms while remaining in the past ('She would be found dead the next morning') or not marked by tense at all ('She died the next morning'). The point here is that prolepsis is entirely relative to an established linear sequence, and therefore cannot be straightforwardly marked by a particular tense. In this regard, narrative reflects the complexity of temporal reference in language more generally. Philosophers and linguists broadly accept that temporal reference is not determined by tense alone, that any single tense, be it past, present or future, is capable of expressing past time, present time and future time, and therefore that the linguistic expression of time spreads itself throughout the whole of a sentence or a discourse.[7]

If tense is not the solitary basis upon which time reference, and therefore prolepsis, can be defined, we might look to a more relativist account of the relationship between the established temporality of a narrative and its proleptic excursions. Genette refers to these as the 'first narrative' and the 'second narrative' respectively: the first narrative is 'the temporal level of narrative with respect to which an anachrony is defined as such' (1980: 48). This idea of the first and the second narrative, or the established narrative and its anachronies will work better for some novels than for others. In *The Driver's Seat*, Spark establishes a first narrative over two chapters before taking her proleptic excursion to Lise's murder. When she does so, it is a brief excursion, with a duration of the one sentence cited above – less in fact, since the story has reverted to the now of the first narrative even before it is over, to the flight 'now boarding at Gate 14'. Genette's idea of the first narrative and the second narrative work well in the case of *The Driver's Seat* because it obeys a kind of maxim of quantity between the narrative and its anachronies: a certain quantity of narration establishes a base temporality in relation to which the prolepsis is anachronous. To put it simply, it is the first narrative because it comes first and because there is more of it.

'If events a, b, c, figure in the text in the order b, c, a then 'a' is analeptic. If, on the other hand, they appear in the order c, a, b then 'c' would be proleptic.' So claims Rimmon-Kenan in *Narrative Fiction* (1983: 46–7) as an explanation of Genette's use of the distinction. One of the interesting things about this apparently simple scheme is the temporal complication it unleashes in relation to the concept it seeks to define. If we consider the account of Genette's first narrative that I have just offered – that it comes first and there is more of it – this formula presents a problem. It suggests that analepsis requires only that the anachronous event be narrated after events which it precedes in the chronological sequence, and that prolepsis requires only that the anachronous event be narrated before events which chronologically precede it. Let me point to some of the many problems. In the first place, why should we not say of the sequence b, c, a that 'b, c' is proleptic, or of the sequence c, a, b that 'a, b' is analeptic? In other words how do we assign the priority to one section of a narrative which is required for Genette's distinction between the first and second narrative, and which views the first as *Chronos* and the other as anachronous? A second problem is that in the proleptic sequence c, a, b, the proleptic event comes first. Rimmon-Kenan no doubt intends this notation to refer to any three events in a narrative sequence, and not to the first three, but we might consider anyway the question of whether a narrative can begin in the mode of prolepsis. Daphne du Maurier's *Rebecca*, for example, begins as many novels do at the end, that is in the narrator's present in relation to which all the events of the novel are in the past. The anachrony comes first in the sense that the dominant pattern of the first narrative is established by the sheer quantity of the subsequent narrative, so that we can no longer claim that the first narrative comes first. If prolepsis can come first, there are several aspects of its conventional definition that have to be abandoned, such as the idea of flashforward. Taken together these first two objections suggest that the assignment of priority to the first narrative, as I did at the end of the last paragraph, on the basis that it comes first and there is more of it, is arbitrary, and that we might just as well view the majority of *Rebecca*, the events after the first chapter, as narrated in a mode of flashback or analepsis.

I will restrict myself to three further complications for any foundational account of prolepsis. The first problem is that fictional narratives, though often taken to be linear in nature, can rarely achieve a temporal shape that can meaningfully be called linear. Todorov (2000: 137–44) points this out in relation to the genre of detective fiction, a genre normally assumed to manifest the strictest of linear forms. But for Todorov, the temporality of the detective story is a double time – a double movement which is at the same time forwards and backwards, working forwards from the crime through the events of the investigation, and in the process working backwards to reconstruct events which lead up to the crime. We might add to this a related complication, namely that a fictional event will often have a complex temporal structure in which one time locus is embedded inside another. A narrated memory has this structure. It is a mental event located in the narrative's quasi-present and yet its content, when represented in fiction, will function to narrate the past within this quasi-present: the memory holds within it the time of its happening and the time that it recalls. But the narration of a memory is not quite the same thing as the narration of the past in the sense that it is not the past itself that is the object of narration but the subjective act of recall belonging to a character. The narration of a memory is not strictly speaking an anachrony, since the event of recalling might belong in the temporal chain of the first narrative, and yet memory is normally considered to be the predominant mode of analepsis. In Virginia Woolf's *Mrs Dalloway*, for example, the events of a single day are narrated according to a rigorous linearity, but because the majority of these events are memories, the narration also entails constant flashback. Analepsis delivered in this mode is not really an anachrony at all, but the effect is anachronous because of the complex temporal structure of the events being narrated.

If the analysis of tense has illustrated the complexity of temporal reference in language, it is unsurprising that this complexity should be manifest in the structure of narration. Prolepsis is meaningful in its narratological sense only when there is a clear first narration in relation to which a flashforward can be seen as anachronous, when that first narrative is predominant. In many narratives in the first person, or which are heavily focalised through a character, the anachronies belong to the thought processes of those dramatised in the fiction. In more experimental fiction, this distinction between the linear narration of thought processes which are not linear, and non-linear narration as such begins to disappear. Tom Crick, the narrator of Graham Swift's *Waterland*, takes the view that any account of the here and now must constantly refer back to a history which produced it, and at the same time refer forwards to events which lie in wait, as part of that history. Though the novel focuses on a single event, the murder of Freddie Parr in 1937, the narration of this event entails many thousands of years of prehistory and about forty years of posthistory which reside in this moment. But prolepsis in *Waterland* is not anachronous in relation to any first narrative because the narrator simply cannot stick with any part of the narrative long enough to establish its priority. *Waterland* is not a novel that can be clearly enough divided into past, present and future to make the idea of prolepsis meaningful, and anticipation occurs in almost every sentence of the narrative. There is an appetite for the kind of temporal complexity I described above, so that anticipation can be embedded even in acts of distant recall: 'Once upon a time there was a future history teacher's wife who, though she said to the future history teacher they should never meet again, married him three years later' (2002: 122). This structure, of prolepsis embedded within analepsis, allows the narrator to circle the event of Freddie Parr's murder, simultaneously narrating events which precede and follow it.

Waterland is a novel that explicitly thematises the forward and backward movement of time, the idea of a cyclical time, and the constitution of the present as a crossed structure of protentions and retentions. But this level of explicit engagement with time is not a necessary condition for a novel to subvert Genette's notion of the first narrative. The same can be said of Robert Coover's *The Babysitter* which empties the idea of prolepsis of its narratological meaning through a kind of 'cut up' technique whereby the narrative jumps constantly in time, so that the principal hermeneutic activity of the reader is the reconstruction of a chronological sequence of events. The effect of subversion is more apparent in the case of novels narrated in backwards time, where prolepsis functions not as an excursion into as yet unknown events, but into past events which are known to the reader from general history, such as the trepidations felt by Tod Friendly in Martin Amis's *Time's Arrow* as he proceeds backwards into the Second World War. The effects of backwards time will be the subject of a fuller discussion later in this book. For the moment the import of these examples is the dependency they illustrate of prolepsis on a conventional and established narrative pattern in which a basic linearity of events is assumed, or on the predominance of chronology over anachrony.

The final problem presented to the narratological meaning of prolepsis is one of knowing when to draw the line between an anachrony or excursion into the future and the kind of plot inference that narratives invite constantly as they proceed. Is a hint, for example, a prolepsis? *The Driver's Seat* opens by referring implicitly forwards to the scene of Lise's murder, and to her own careful staging of that scene, by showing Lise in the act of rejecting a dress made in a fabric which will not stain. Lise, who seeks to control in advance even the photographs of her own dead body, needs a fabric that will show blood, but as we read this opening scene, the motivation which underlies this rejection of the non-staining fabric is not apparent to us. This idea of motivation, of some psychological intent which is not apparent at first, but which unfolds with the plot, is clearly a central device in the forward motion of narrative. So common is this kind of hint, or invited inference, that we normally assume that early events are only narrated if they will acquire significance later that is not apparent at the time of their occurrence. In other words, an actual excursion into the future events of a narrative is not required for the production of teleological retrospect, and we find ourselves projecting forward in the act of reading to envisage the future significance of events as a basic process in the decoding of the narrative present. Nor is the idea of motivation necessarily a hidden psychological intent. Tomachevsky (1971) outlined a kind of technical sense of motivation, according to which the presence of a gun at the beginning of a narrative anticipates the murder or suicide of one the characters later in the plot. This is a plot device which is followed up by Sartre (1969) and then by Barthes (1968), and again this kind of anticipation, or invited inference, is complicated in relation to prolepsis. Clearly the presence of a gun invites the inference that it is a motivated object in terms of the plot, but as Beckett's *Happy Days*, and hundreds of so-called 'red herrings' in detective fiction confirm, the inference is often mistaken. Barthes hedges his bets on this question by providing an alternative account of the presence of objects in narrative based not on motivation but on redundancy. An object such as the barometer which hangs on the wall of Mme. Aubain's room in Flaubert's 'Un Coeur Simple' may be viewed as redundant detail which works in the service of a reality effect, and whose only motivation is the claim that this is the kind of object that would be found in a house like this. Edgar Allan Poe's 'The Cask of Amontillado' puns on the word 'mason' as a foreshadowing of the fate of its character to be bricked up in a recess of the wine cellar, but the pun functions as prolepsis only because it turns out to be motivated. How then are we to distinguish between in the first place the motivated object or event and the red herring, and in the second place between motivated and redundant details? It seems to make no sense in relation to any definition of prolepsis to say that any hint of a future event in a narrative is proleptic. Are we then to say that an event or object is proleptic only when it anticipates an event which does indeed confer significance on it, and not so when it turns out to be a red herring or an instance of redundant detail?

Performative Prolepsis and Self-subverting Prophecy

We seem to have arrived, in this list of complications, at a rather circular account of prolepsis, namely that the anticipation of future events in a fiction counts as prolepsis only when that anticipation turns out to be true. This is to say that the narratological context of Prolepsis 1 is not properly named as anticipation at all, since anticipation itself requires no verification in relation to the future that it anticipates, but requires an actual excursion into the future of narrated events. I began this discussion with the distinction between Prolepsis 1 and Prolepsis 3, or the narratological and rhetorical meanings of the word. But if the narratological sense of prolepsis depends in some way on true prognostication, how can we then connect it with the rhetorical sense which, as I defined it at the start, seems to aim precisely at the preclusion of the event anticipated, namely the anticipation of an objection to an argument. If Prolepsis 1 is verifiable in relation to an existing fictional future, Prolepsis 3 is orientated towards the non-existence in the future of the future it anticipates. It follows that neither Prolepsis 1 nor Prolepsis 3 can have any real existence in life, since in the first case the future to which it refers can only have existence in a fictional world, in which futures are always already determined and lie in wait, whereas Prolepsis 3 prevents the future it anticipates in the act of anticipating it.

At the start of this discussion I linked Prolepsis 2 with the preterite tense of classical narration, which is to say that it is a form of anticipation which takes place between the time locus of the narrated and the time locus of the narrator. The preterite tense has this anticipation built into it in the sense that the events of narration are only narrated in the past tense at all because they are past in relation to this time locus of the narrator, or what Ricoeur calls the time of narrating. There is a sense then in which the present of a narrative is structurally retrospective, or actually structured in relation to the future present from which it is narrated. This is to be distinguished from an actual proleptic excursion from narrated time to the time of narrating, a kind of flashforward which abounds in fiction. This latter kind of excursion can be found whenever a narrator intrudes into narrated events to remind a reader of the time locus of narrating, such as the intrusive narrators of Fielding, the excesses of self-consciousness of Tristram Shandy's self-narration, in a considerable number of novels of the nineteenth century, in Conrad's leaps forward to storytelling situations in which narrators and listeners are dramatised on ships, and in many metafictional experiments in the novels of the late-twentieth century. Many of these temporal relations in fiction between narrated time and the time of narrating will be the object of systematic analysis later in this study. For the moment I want to concentrate on the first idea, not that a narrative might flashforward by leaving the time locus of narrated events, but that the moment of the present might be structured by an anticipation of the retrospect of the time of narrating.

It is true that the preterite tense gives the present of a fictional narrative a relation with a future present from which it will be viewed retrospectively. It was my proposition at the start of this chapter that the decoding of the preterite in the act of reading fiction was a kind of presentification, of making present, that which is in the past and that this presentification corresponds to a process of depresentification which might take place outside of fiction. This analytical model, which depends on the inside and the outside of fiction is not one that can easily be defended, as the later sections of this book will make clear, but at present it offers a hypothesis that will take me in the direction of those sections. How then might the present be structured as a future narration of the past outside of fiction? One answer to this question is simply that the present can be conceived and even lived in a mode of narration in the past. I might, for example, leave the house while saying to myself 'Mark left the house'. A more probable instance would be a less banal situation which I intended to narrate later – perhaps an event which takes place without witnesses that I know I will recount. Experiences which take place overseas, for example, are often lived in a mode of anticipation of the act of narrating them afterwards. They are recorded in the present as if recounted in the past. The present is experienced as the object of a future memory, or in anticipation of retrospection. The depresentification of this mode is well known as a kind of schizophrenia involved in the act of self-narration: when an experience becomes both the subject and the object of a narration. If my lived present is translated into the conventional preterite of fictional narrative, there is a temporal depresentification involved in the transformation of present into past. There is also a spatial self-distance, or depresentification, involved in the translation of first person pronouns into the third person, as when 'I' becomes 'Mark' in 'Mark left the house'. I see myself as somebody else, and I see myself from a temporal distance, and in this double act of depresentification I split myself into two both spatially and temporally. Nor is this mode of depresentification confined to a mode of verbal narration. In fact the self-recording and self-archiving involved in this kind of schizophrenic self-narration may have become predominantly visual as photography and video recording have displaced verbal narration, and film and television have come to occupy the place of fiction in the hermeneutic circle between narrative and life.

Video recording and photography, like the preterite tense, structure the present as the object of a future memory. The act of recording installs in the present an anticipated future from which the present will be re-experienced as representation of the past, or an infinite sequence of future presents from which the moment can be recollected. In digital photography, the effect is one of foreshortening the present, since the image is consumed almost instantly, consigning the present of a few moments ago to the past and inaugurating an infinite sequence of future presents from which that moment will be represented as past. Similarly, digital video often involves the repetition of a sequence as recording at the moment that the recording stops, creating an instant nostalgia for the very recent past. In Derrida's writings on the archive, on archive fever and the process of archivisation, he goes further than this. As I argued in Chapter 2, the archive is not to be understood as a record of the past, but as a temporal mode in which moments exist only for the purposes of archivisation:

> the technical structure of the archiving archive also determines the structure of the archivable content even in its very coming into existence and in its relationship to the future. The archivization produces as much as it records the event. This is also our political experience of the so-called news media. (1996: 17)

Just as the personal present is produced by its own future, by the possibility of representing it later, so too are our most collective moments, as represented for example, by television news. The relevance of technology here, as Derrida makes clear in *Archive Fever* (Derrida 1998), is that the archiving process is accelerated to a speed of near instantaneity, through a technological modernity. It is reasonable to believe in the context of this technology that in personal and collective terms, we increasingly experience the present as the object of a future memory.

There are two ideas here that I would like to dwell on. The first is the idea that technology accelerates the sequence of present and the future from which it is to be represented to a point of near instantaneity; the second is the idea that the future actively produces the event that it purports to record, or to passively represent. I would like to use it to illustrate what Derrida means when he says that 'Deconstruction is America' (2002: xxiv). The perplexing thing about this claim is that it seems to link a complex philosophical discourse with a complex social entity, or to claim that the identity of one is the identity of the other. The link can be made in the following way. One of the recurring logics, or rather disruptions to classical logic, at work in deconstruction as Derrida practices it, is the logic of supplementarity. This is a kind of temporal loop by which things which happen later in a sequence are understood as the origins of things from which they apparently originate. In *Speech and Phenomena*, the logic of this 'strange structure' is expressed thus: 'a possibility produces that to which it is said to be added on' (1973: 89). If we apply this logic to the case of the digital video recording, its structure becomes apparent, since the event being recorded often comes into being only as a recording, or as something to be remembered. So too in television news, the sequence of event and its representation, in which priority is assigned to the event and a secondary role to the representation of that event, cannot be maintained in the case of a soundbite, or a terrorist act. The beheading of a hostage in Iraq, for example is an event produced by the possibility that it will be represented, so that the representation cannot be viewed as secondary. The logic of supplementarity makes the anticipation of retrospection into a first cause, which precedes the event it purports to follow. Supplementarity is not the only strange structure at work in the operations of deconstruction but it is in my view the one that best explains it; and supplementarity is not the only characteristic of American society, of its individual and collective consciousnesses, but it offers a compelling image of its changing experience of time.

Might we then also say that the structure of supplementarity is the structure of prolepsis? Derrida constantly warns against the metaphysics of the 'is' in an equation such as 'Deconstruction is America': the 'is' carries no imputation of identity, and particularly not in a way that can be removed from the context of a particular discourse. In this cavalier spirit it probably is possible to claim that prolepsis is supplementarity. Though prolepsis is normally assumed, at least in its narratological context, to name an excursion forwards in a sequence, this excursion seems to be a journey to somewhere which precedes the point of departure. This is particularly clear in the case of the structural prolepsis of the preterite, since the anticipated retrospect of the time of narrating forms the grammar of the event to be narrated. The same thing happens if I go to India so that I won't regret not going, or because I want to have been, or because I envisage the stories of adventure that I might tell. A possible future produces the event to which it is said to be added on, or the archive produces the event as much as it records it.

Yet it would be nonsensical to say that the future precedes the present. The temporal structure involved here needs to be given a clearer definition. In terms of cause and effect, what might we identify from the future as a cause of an event in the present? I think the answer to this question lies in the phrasing of Derrida's account of the strange structure of the supplement as a possibility which produces that to which it is said to be added on. The cause in this temporal chain is not an actual future, but a possibility, or an envisaged future. As an envisaged future, it is not properly thought of as future at all, and conforms more closely to what Husserl (1964) terms a protention: a part of the present which is future orientated. Whereas it might be an affront to the tidy mind to think that a future event can precede or cause an event in the present, the idea that a protention, or the projection forward to a possible future, might do so ought to be perfectly acceptable. In the case of a soundbite, for example, a speaker might imagine a form of words irresistible to the news editor, might envisage the repeated events of their actual broadcast, or the contexts of their reception. But these are imagined futures, not future events. The logic of supplementarity, as it operates in Derrida's work, and in deconstruction more widely, often borrows some melodrama from the obfuscation of this difference, implying that the linearity of time is somehow denied by this most mundane of mind operations, the protention.

But there is more to be said on the subject of the causal protention than this, which will help us to characterise prolepsis more generally. Derrida reminds us constantly that in this situation, and in language more generally, we post things out into the future on the basis of a kind of promise, but amid the possibility that things will go wrong, that our messages may not be received, or that the futures that we have envisaged may not come about. Put simply, there are two futures, the future that we envisage correctly, and the future that comes out of nowhere. But whereas in fiction, the future may be lying in wait for us, in life it is not, so that the idea of futures correctly or incorrectly envisaged cannot be meaningful. It might be better to say that there are those that we successfully bring into being and those that we unsuccessfully bring into being. In the case of a soundbite, the future event which shapes the form of words of the attention-seeking politician may or may not take place. If the soundbite is reported, its formulation has successfully produced the event of its representation, and this might be thought of more accurately as the successful production of, rather than the correct anticipation of, an event. To use the language of speech act theory, the soundbite is a performative, in the sense that it constitutes, or brings into existence a state of affairs.

A performative prolepsis takes an excursion into the future to envisage an event which produces the present in such a way that the envisaged future actually comes about. Philosophy has known this loop as the self-fulfilling prophecy, but has not analysed it in any detail. The self-fulfilling prophecy tends to be viewed as an exceptional or deviant case, which applies only to the most explicitly prophetic statements. One of the possible consequences of my argument is that the idea of prophecy will require to be extended to encompass many more language situations than the prophetic statement, just as the performative of speech act theory has acquired an infinitely extended scope.[8] It is possible to view Derrida's treatment of Husserl's notion of protention, or the concept of *différance* as a claim that all language exists in a condition of waiting to find out if its prophecies are fulfilled or not. A performative prolepsis involves an imagined future which produces the present, and a present which, thus produced, produces the future. As such it is the most common relation of the present to the future, the one which pertains in repetition, automatic perception, and self-narration, in which the future turns out as expected. It is what Derrida calls the Messianic future, the unpredicted, unforeseeable future,[9] which is more properly thought of as the exception, the deviant case of the performative prolepsis that goes wrong.

Performative prolepsis produces the future in the act of envisaging it, so that the possible transforms itself into the actual. It does so in a range of modes and moods which can be placed somewhere on a scale between fear and hope. These two modes of protention, fear and hope, clearly operate as much in the reading of a fictional narrative as they do in the everyday projections we make into the future, in our realisations and evasions of fearful outcomes, or our fulfilled and dashed hopes. But what does this tell us about the distinction that we started from in this discussion – the link between narratological and rhetorical prolepsis? One approach to this question is to explore the way that the performative prolepsis operates when it produces or fails to produce the future by pre-empting an objection, in other words to look at the successes and failures of rhetorical prolepsis. Something must be said first of the difference between this device in the context of a spoken oration and that of a written discourse, if only to establish the different temporalities involved in speech and writing. The speaker of an oration who anticipates an objection ('You may say that I am unpatriotic, but I say to you . . .') addresses someone who is present, who may or may not have formulated such an objection, and who is interpellated into the position of the objector. The potentially objectionable argument, the attempt to preclude the objection, and (if this is successful) its actual preclusion take place in the same time and space. There may be anticipation involved, but it is not anticipation on quite the same temporal scale as would be the case in written discourse, where the act of anticipation must traverse the gap between the time of writing and the time of reading. This is significant for two reasons: that the gap between the time of writing and reading is in theory almost infinitely large, making the act of anticipation less certain and the interpellation of unknown readers less guaranteed; and because the formulation of a response to writing takes place in a more considered context, in which the time of responding lies in the control of the reader and not the writer. For these reasons it is reasonable to think that the interpellation of a reader into the position of the objector and the subsequent preclusion of that objection ought to be considerably less manageable in writing than in speech, and the performative of the prolepsis involved (the preclusion of objection) therefore less likely to succeed.

The written version of this kind of anticipation has become one of the most prominent characteristics of contemporary writing.[10] But it has not always been adequately understood or analysed. In relation to contemporary fiction, for example, a discourse which anticipates an objection has been understood in recent years under the rubric of the term 'metafiction', that is as self-conscious fiction. In the discussion so far we have already made the connection between time and self-consciousness in several ways, particularly in relation to the kind of prolepsis which involves an experience of the present as the object of a future memory, in the digital video camera, for example, but also in Prolepsis 2, where a narration travels forwards from narrated time to the time of the narrative as a mode of fictional self-consciousness. One of the weaknesses of academic criticism is that, though it has been preoccupied with the issue of self-consciousness, it has never dealt with the issue of self-consciousness in relation to time, or with the help of the philosophy of time, which has always held these topics together in a productive relationship. The need for a philosophy of time became more obvious after the arrival of the concepts of postmodernism in criticism and philosophy. It is now commonplace, for example, to hear the postmodern novel defined as 'historiographic metafiction', which is to say self-conscious fiction which raises questions about the knowability of the past and its representation if fictional form. Metafiction is normally understood as Patricia Waugh describes it, as 'writing which consistently displays its conventionality, which explicitly and overtly lays bare its condition of artifice, and which thereby explores the problematic relationship between life and fiction' (1984: 4). It belongs to an era in which readers are distrustful of fiction, it acknowledges that its productions are not true and incorporates the anticipated resistance to the referential illusion into the fiction itself. It is *postmodernist*, in this respect, because it assumes a reader conditioned by the experiments of Modernist fiction to notice and resist the conventions at work in the production of fictional reference. If a prolepsis is performative when it brings about the future that it anticipates, the metafiction is one of its instances, incorporating an anticipated critical response into the discourse being responded to. When John Fowles's authorial interventions remind the reader of *The French Lieutenant's Woman* that the novel's characters are figments of his imagination, it seems to try to preclude and appropriate such a response in a reader: the knowing distanced response which refuses to yield to the referential illusion. The reader, like the members of an orator's audience addressed by the rhetorical prolepsis, is interpellated into a position of suspicious distrust, or of uncooperation, or resistance to fictional protocols. Should the reader oblige and adopt such a position, a certain rhetorical aim will have been achieved, namely agreement. In the act of siding with the resistant reader, the fictional discourse has dissociated itself from the fiction which is the object of suspicion, and secured agreement between the discourse and the reader.

Of course this may not work. The reader accustomed to such a ploy (perhaps after more than three decades of fiction which appropriates and uses the reader's suspicion towards fiction as a reliable medium for historical knowledge against him) may well resist the interpellation, and therefore resist the resistance. But what does it mean to resist the resistance, or rather to refuse the position of dissent into which a discourse such as a metafiction interpellates us? The effects of this are clearest in commercial advertising, where the rhetorical designs of the reader are most base and palpable, but where the act of persuasion often entails the advertisement's self-distance, or distance from itself and the act of persuasion that it advances. A clear example of this kind of anti-advertising is French Connection's FCUK campaign which has been running in Britain for several years. The slogan FCUK ADVERTISING, for example, offers as its primary meaning and as its alibi, the name of the company and therefore names the publicity wing of that company. Even before we decode FCUK as 'fuck', this is a self-referential advert: it names the advert rather than the product. It is equivalent not to a slogan that says 'Drink Coca-Cola', but one that says 'Coca-Cola Promotions'. It therefore does not seek to hide its function as a promotion, but to highlight it. It is like a sign which says 'sign' or a novel called 'A Novel'. At this level it is tempting to view the advert as a peculiarly literal message, though strictly speaking I think it is not literal: the literal act of self-designation would be 'FCUK ADVERT', whereas 'FCUK Advertising' is a metonymy insofar as it names the larger entity, the advertising campaign, of which this is an instance or a part. The slogan therefore has the kind of doubleness that the word 'language' shares, namely the double designation of itself and the larger whole to which it belongs. But this primary meaning or alibi as Barthes would have it, is a thin layer, and it could be argued, not really primary at all, since the most immediate impact of the slogan is the transposition of two letters to produce the most feeble of anagrams. Taken together, the message which names itself and the advertising campaign to which it belongs interact with a message which directs verbal abuse towards the whole activity of advertising, finding its humour in the feeble transparency of its alibi – the message which establishes its legitimacy in literal and metonymic self-naming. This, at least is one way of reading the other side of the visual pun: the rude rejection of advertising. There is possibly another interpretation which would see a corporation declaring that it has no need to advertise. Either way, the message produces a contradiction between the act of advertising and either the wholesale rejection of advertising or the declaration that it is unnecessary. The question then becomes, how can an advertisement operate as persuasion and at the same time claim this kind of aggressive opposition to the act of persuasion that it advances?

A minimal survey of the terrain of contemporary advertising will show that this question is framed the wrong way round. The performative contradiction involved in 'FCUK ADVERTISING' is not a deviant example but a paradigm for the way that this mode of persuasion operates. It does so attempting to preclude an objection to the rhetoric of advertising by anticipating it, or through the device of rhetorical prolepsis. As in the case of the metafiction, the anti-advertisement works by interpellating the reader into a position of suspicious distrust and using that distrust as a way of selling something. In this case the distrust is of a general kind, directed towards the entire culture of advertising. Whereas the resistance to advertising traditionally entails the rejection of its forms of persuasion, in the case of the FCUK slogan, that resistance has been appropriated by the advertisement itself. The suspicious reader, therefore, finds that resistance is not something which separates him from the rhetoric of the advertisement, but actually places him in agreement with its message. If one of the messages of this advertisement is 'fuck advertising', to disagree will be to embrace advertising. The association that this establishes is clear: it unites FCUK and the resistant reader against advertising, and while the former continues to be an instance of advertising, the latter continues to be duped by it. Speaking of metafiction's attempts to appropriate the critical response of a reader, Gerald Prince insists that the metanarrative sign succeeds only in specifying the distance between a narrative's attempts at critical self-commentary and the actual response of a given reader (Prince 1982). In other words, the narrative may attempt to anticipate, articulate and pre-empt an objection but this does not pre-empt the objection to that strategy itself. The streetwise reader who has read Naomi Klein's *No Logo* will not be taken in by the anti-advertisement and will see it as another instance of ideological interpellation operating under the disguise of irony or self-distance. It may be in this ultimate powerlessness over the actual response of a given reader that this kind of prolepsis finds its most subtle forms of manipulation. In this case that manipulation works through a structure in which the secondary message 'fuck advertising' seems to contradict the aims of the first 'fcuk advertising', but in which resistance to the self-resistance of the message will result in an embrace of the advertising industry.

FCUK is a kind of algebra for narratological prolepsis (like Rimmon-Kenan's c, a, b) in which 'c' is proleptic: it involves a kind of flashforward to the letter 'c'. But its function as an anti-advertisement, like the metafiction, should be understood in the context of rhetorical prolepsis, as a device which anticipates a general climate of resistance in its readership. Its attempts to appropriate that resistance have become a predominant mode of ideological interpellation. In place of the question of how an advertisement can simultaneously operate as persuasion and oppose that act of persuasion, we might ask how it could do otherwise: is it possible for an advertisement to be effective in this climate of resistance without some gesture towards that resistance? The contradiction, far from being a form of self-subversion, is a special kind of performative. The performative contradiction, in this case and in general, can be viewed in two ways. On one hand it can be viewed as an utterance which says one thing and does another. This is the meaning given to the idea by Habermas when he uses the phrase to suggest that deconstruction cannot advance a position that language cannot convey truth and at the same time expect a reader to take this position to be true. From this point of view the performative contradiction is a kind of inconsistency or fault. On the other hand, it might be viewed as an utterance which is performative in the sense that it brings something, a state of affairs, into being, and in this case that state of affairs is a contradiction. The anti-advertisement, for example, does not make a statement which, like a constative utterance, could be judged true or false, but brings a contradiction into being. This means that it is not a performative in the same way as a video recording, which in the act of anticipating the retrospective view of the present, constructs the present as the memory it will become. The performative of Prolepsis 3 – the anticipation of an objection on the part of a reader – is subject to the vicissitudes of any discourse which is to be interpreted, and its attempts to preclude objection may fall foul to, for example, the misrecognition of the audience, as when *Tristram Shandy* is read a thousand years after its writing, or the FCUK advert is decoded in Bhutan. There is a sense in which the metafiction and the anti-advertisement implant an objection in the mind of a reader, and perhaps with the motive of diverting attention from the most feared objections, and this implantation will therefore work in a performative way. But as Prince's account of the metanarrative sign reminds us, this is never performative in the sense of being a straightforward determination of the response of a given reader. The excursion that Prolepsis 3 takes into the future is an excursion into the unforeseeable.

Here, it is necessary to return to the principal argumentative project of this chapter, which is to articulate the connection between the narratological and the rhetorical meanings of the word prolepsis. In the case of Prolepsis 1, in which the time travel takes place within the boundaries of narrated time, the future is predetermined, literally already written, and lying in wait. In the case of Prolepsis 2, the future is successfully brought into being by the act of anticipation, because the archive produces the event it purports to record. In the case of Prolepsis 3, the performativity of an anticipation is an attempt, mostly doomed to fail, to preclude objection, and the actual future time locus involved is indeterminate and unforeseeable. In relation to time, this is how the hermeneutic circle of presentification and depresentification works: Prolepsis 1, with its Godlike power to visit the future, instructs us in teleological retrospect, with the effect that it encourages us to narrate our lives in the preterite, looking back on the present from envisaged future moments, in the manner of Prolepsis 2. This mode of experience, with all of its technological support, installs in the present a temporal self-distance which operates in a mode of storytelling. This temporal self-distance also operates in Prolepsis 3, in which the message contains within it protentions towards an imagined objection of the other, with a view to forestalling that objection. Seen from the point of view of rhetorical manipulation or as ideological interpellation, Prolepsis 3 borrows something of the apparent neutrality of Prolepses 1 and 2, confusing the boundary between the sender and the receiver of a message with the neutrality of that between the present and the future. The relationship of Prolepsis 1 and Prolepsis 3 is therefore the axis between time and self-consciousness, since storytelling is not just self-distance but temporal self-distance, and on this subject, narratology has much to learn from the philosophy of time.

Notes

1. See, for example, *Being and Time* sections 53 and 64 (pp. 304–11; 352–8). Heidegger's account of anticipation is the subject of fuller discussion in Chapter 4 below.

2. 'Future anterior' is a phrase borrowed from Derrida's *Of Grammatology* p. 5 to indicate a future which comes before as well as a past which will exist in the future.

3. This is a term used by Ricoeur in *Time and Narrative*, but which he borrows from Muller. See Ricoeur, Vol. 2, p. 78. Compare Heidegger's term 'presencing' which is used to mean something like Augustine's notion of distension: the inclusion of the past and future within the present. For a discussion see Simms (2003: 82).

4. The phrasing here is taken from Heidegger's discussion of anticipation in *Being and Time*, p. 444.

5. Genette uses the distinction between internal prolepsis and external prolepis in *Narrative Discourse* but it is also worth pointing out here that the crossing of diegetic levels in fiction of this kind is also designated by the term 'metalepsis'. Also Heise's *Chronoschisms* p. 24 uses 'metalepsis' to identify this crossing as one the characteristics of temporality in the postmodern novel.

6. See for example Derrida, *Positions*.

7. For an accessible discussion of the complexity of tense and time reference see Crystal 2002. For a more complex discussion see McGilvray 1991.

8. For a discussion of the extended scope of the performative in literary studies, see Culler 1997: 95–109.

9. See Derrida 1995: 54.

10. The discussion that follows of rhetorical prolepsis in writing focuses on fiction, but it is clearly a recurrent feature of academic writing. Peggy Kamuf highlights this in a negative assessment of the strategy in *Without Alibi*, p. 7: 'But why anticipate, why call up resistance? It's a familiar tactic; we've all used it many times – to respond in advance to imagined or anticipated objections, as if one could conquer the other's resistance before it has even had a chance to manifest itself. Many books are written almost entirely in this mode of preconquered resistance, which usually makes them quite unreadable' (Derrida 2002: 7).

Chapter 4

Temporality and Self-Distance

The Future is already; otherwise how could my love be love?
(Sartre 1969: 165)

One of the things that narrative theory can learn from philosophy is a proper sense of the importance of the future. I have suggested several times already that narrative theory shows a preoccupation with memory, retrospect and the archiving of past events, and has an undeveloped potential to address questions about the present and future. The significance of the notions of 'anticipation' and 'prolepsis' is that, in different ways, they refer to this relation between the present and actual or possible futures. With philosophy as its teacher, narrative theory can turn its attention to narrative not only in its function as archive, but to the question of narrative as a mode of being.

In Heidegger's account of being, for example, the future is the all important tense. Like Derrida, Heidegger tends to view things normally understood as secondary and derivative as primary and primordial, and so it is with the relationship between time (Zeit) and temporality (Zeitlichkeit) in *Being and Time*. If, for a moment, we view time as a mind-independent entity and temporality as the experience of time in consciousness, or time within the condition of being, it might normally be assumed that the latter derives from the former. According to Heidegger, there is a conception of time as a series of 'nows' which is shared by ordinary people and philosophers from Aristotle to Bergson. These philosophers and ordinary people will view time, with its fundamental terminology of 'past', 'present' and 'future' as a primordial entity from which the human experience of time is derived. For Heidegger, it is the other way around: temporality is a mode of being from which the concept of time is derived. In simple terms, time is not something which exists in the world and is then reflected in the human mind, but something which arises from human being (Dasein) and is then projected onto the world. According to this view, it is a mistake to think that human minds passively experience the time of the outside world. For Heidegger, 'world-time', like the concept of time in general, is actively produced by human modes of being which subsequently temporalise our sense of the outside world. This is in fact what temporality is: it is the process of temporalising. As Heidegger puts it, 'it is not an entity at all. It is not, but it temporalizes . . . Temporality temporalizes' (377). This is in itself an important characteristic of Heidegger's contribution to the philosophy of time, but it also helps to understand how the future comes to occupy a dominant position in his account of being. If 'time' and 'world-time' are mere derivatives from human temporality, rather than the other way around, the traditional account of 'past', 'present' and 'future', tensed as that which did exist, does exist and will exist, can no longer function as the foundational framework for time:

> In our terminological use of this expression (temporality), we must hold ourselves aloof from all those significations of 'future', 'past' and 'Present' which thrust themselves upon us from the ordinary conception of time. This holds also for conceptions of a 'time' which is 'subjective' or 'Objective', 'immanent' or 'transcendent'. Inasmuch as Dasein understands itself in a way which, proximally and for the most part, is inauthentic, we may suppose that 'time' as ordinarily understood does not represent a genuine phenomenon, but one which is derivative [ein abkünftiges]. It arises from inauthentic temporality, which has a source of its own. The conceptions of 'future', 'past' and 'Present' have first arisen in terms of the inauthentic way of understanding time. (1962: 374)

Several of our key analytical concepts are here consigned to a secondary and derivative position: the framework of past, present and future, the distinction of objective and subjective time, and the conceptions of immanent and transcendent time which have dominated since Kant. Heidegger also claims that it is from inauthentic temporality that time is derived, meaning that it derives from a kind of passive human experience of time as an endless sequence. Authentic temporality on the other hand is a more active, decisive, and self-owned relation to time, one which knows that time, for Being, is finite, and crucially, one which can project forward to Death, in the mode that Heidegger refers to as Being-towards-death. The critical question therefore becomes: what is an authentic and primordial temporality? The answer is variously offered by Heidegger, as Care, Being-towards-death, and Being itself, all of which offer associated aspects of this active and decisive relation to time. He also calls this relation 'anticipatory resoluteness', a phrase which carries within it the whole chain of associations which comprise authentic and primordial temporality.

Anticipatory resoluteness is authentic Being, and as anticipation, its orientation is towards the future. There is also an inauthentic way of relating to the future, just as there is both an authentic and an inauthentic way of relating to the present and the past.[1] But the most important aspect of temporality is that the dimensions of past, present and future, which Heidegger calls ecstases, are unified so that Being has a triadic structure. Authentic Being will project forward to death and backwards to birth and beyond as a way of understanding how to act, and from this point of view the present is always structured, or temporalised. Inauthentic being will tend to lose itself in presence, or pay heed only to the immediate past and future in the contemplation of the present situation. In authentic Being, there is always a projection forwards to death, towards the end of being, or towards what Heidegger calls 'the possibility we have characterized as Dasein's utter impossibility' (1962: 378), in such a way that Being sees itself as authentically whole, and finite. The authentic future, or perhaps the authentic way of relating to the future, is 'temporalized primarily by that temporality which makes up the meaning of anticipatory resoluteness' (1962: 378). This chain of associations, of authenticity, anticipation, resoluteness and Being-towards-death make up the future aspect of the ecstatic temporality of being. This is not a future that we wait for, but a process of temporalising which involves the 'unity of the ecstases', in other words the triadic structure of being. Heidegger insists constantly on the equiprimordiality of the ecstases, and yet, at the same time, insists on the priority of the future:

> In enumerating the ecstases, we have always mentioned the future first. We have done this to indicate that the future has a priority in the ecstatical unity of primordial and authentic temporality. This is so even though temporality does not first arise through a cumulative sequence of the ecstases, but in each case temporalizes itself in their equiprimordiality. But within this equiprimordiality, the modes of temporalization are different. The difference lies in the fact that the nature of the temporalizing can be determined primarily in terms of the different ecstases. Primordial and authentic temporality temporalizes itself in terms of the authentic future and in such a way that in having been futurally, it first of all awakens the Present. *The primary phenomenon of primordial and authentic temporality is the future.* (1962: 378)

So it is not that the future comes first. This cannot be what 'priority' means, since there is no sequence. Rather, the three ecstases of past, present and future are all in operation at the same time whenever temporality temporalises. And yet whenever it does so authentically it always does so 'in terms of' the authentic future, in other words the scouting forward to Death in a mode of anticipatory resoluteness as described above, and therefore it 'first of all awakens' the present. There is a contradiction here, and it contains a tautology. The contradiction is that having said that the future does not come first, or have priority in any temporal sense, a clear temporal priority is assigned to the future by the phrase 'first of all awakens'. The tautology is that within the equiprimordial unity of the ecstases, the future has priority because it comes first, which is a repetition, not an explanation. It might be argued that this is not temporal priority but conceptual priority, or that conceptual priority is being expressed through the metaphor of temporal priority, in which case the charge can be modified from that of contradiction to that of irresponsible choice of metaphor. Alternatively, and perhaps more sophisticatedly, it might be thought that it is the very inseparability of conceptual and temporal priority that authentic temporality designates, but if this is so, the charge of tautology must stand over any claim which bases the conceptual priority of the future in its temporal priority or vice versa.[2]

In the spirit of the idea that the contradictions and tautologies of Heidegger's writing are inherent in the modes of being he describes, to be thought of as strengths rather than flaws, it could be said that the triadic structure of past, present and future represents a system which is nothing other than a tautology masquerading as an analytical distinction. How can one give definition to any of the three terms in this system without merely defining it negatively in relation to the other two: the past is that which was present, the present is that which will be past and was future, etc. Semiology has encouraged us to think of such signs as having no content other than these systematic relations, so that the idea of the present is actually constituted by the past and future, and has no positive content of its own. In this light, Heidegger's idea of temporality as the unification of ecstases might be thought of as a recognition of this kind of inseparability and mutual constitution. Heidegger constantly reminds us in *Being and Time* to discard the ordinary conception of time, which would encourage us to think of the present as the only domain of existence and being. And why must it be discarded? Because every time we look analytically at the present, we find it divided by, indeed constituted by, relations to the past and the future. Hence, in his discussion of the present, the inauthentic relation is that of 'making present', or constructing the illusion of being present-at-hand, while the authentic one is the relation which Heidegger refers to in the phrase 'the moment of vision', that is a present which envisages the future by projecting forwards. The inauthentic relation to the present is the one which, in the act of 'making present', denies the constitutive role of the past and future in the present, while the authentic relation envisages, and therefore highlights, the future. This is very interesting for my purposes, for a number of reasons. The first is that it is clearly consonant with the idea we have already discussed in relation to Derrida – that the present thought of in the ordinary way as 'now' is less authentic than the idea of the present as divided between past and future, and in particular, the present as anticipation. Given the mutual co-implication and constitution of the three ecstases, there is no reason to privilege one above another, since each is included in the others. For Heidegger and Derrida, this condition of reasonlessness provides a reason, which is that the traditional privilege accorded to the present must be strategically opposed, since it can have no basis, and therefore functions as a presupposition. This view of the unity of past, present and future, whether derived from ecstatic unity or semiological relationism, provides a defence against the charge of contradiction and tautology. The contradiction between the equiprimordiality of the ecstases and the priority of the future is merely the difference between a temporal/conceptual priority and a strategic priority tilted against the presupposition of undivided presence, while the tautology is merely the expression of the mutually constitutive role of signs.

There is a second reason that Heidegger's rejection of the present is of particular relevance to me. The authentic relation to the present, we have seen, is the 'moment of vision', in other words, the event in the present which projects forward into the future. The inauthentic relation to the present is 'making present'. The hermeneutic circle with which I have been working proposes an act of reading which consists in the presentification of the past, and a mode of being which consists in the projection forward to a future which looks back on the present. In Heidegger's terms, the first is the inauthentic present, or making present, while the second is the authentic present, or moment of vision. If the central idea of the hermeneutic circle is that the two activities, or modes, produce each other, we must accept that in Heidegger's framework, this involves the mutual production of authentic and inauthentic temporalities. What I have been calling the 'presentification' which is involved in the decoding of narrative fiction is not exactly what Heidegger means, most of the time, by 'making present'. Nevertheless, the basic process involved in the inauthentic ecstasis of the present is that of either isolating presence from the unity of the ecstases, or privileging it, as a way of upholding presence as the basic condition of being, and this must also be the activity of reading when past events are, to use Heidegger's phrase, made present-at-hand: the character of events as 'having been', which is encoded in their tense, is simply decoded as presence.

Heidegger's notion of authenticity adds an interesting dimension to the hermeneutic circle of reading and being. But authenticity is much more, in *Being and Time*, than rejecting presence in favour of the future.

Authenticity is deeply bound up with individuation, and with self-ownership and these characteristics of authentic being are linked to the future partly through death. Being-towards-death brings authenticity to Dasein not only in the form of a sense of finite wholeness to life, but also for its intense perspective on the ownership of Dasein. Because nobody can do my dying for me, Being-towards-death reminds me that nobody can do my living for me either, and therefore offers me an intensified individuation and sense of ownership over my Dasein. What this means, for our purposes, is that the reading of fiction involves not one but two fundamentally inauthentic processes. I have just suggested that the process of 'making present' in Heidegger and the presentification of reading fiction share a condition of inauthenticity as modes of being. Now there is another source of inauthenticity, namely the vicarious nature of fictional experience. In reading a fiction, I am normally engaged in the construction of presence where there is none, but I am also letting someone else do my living for me. In this tradition of phenomenology it is always dangerous to assume that authenticity is simply a positive value and inauthenticity a negative one, and for this reason, the argument here is not simply pointing to the conclusion that there is something bad in the reading of fiction. Having said that, in both Heidegger and Sartre, there is a complex network of evaluative terms at work in the description of inauthenticity – of negativity, everydayness, fallenness, nothingness, bad faith, tranquillisation, alienation, etc. Even if it pretends otherwise, and regularly resorts to this 'otherwise' as an alibi, the description is an evaluation, and therefore, since authenticity is structured as a future-oriented project, such a project is presented as a superior form of understanding. This is a complicated issue, and the current project does not allow an adequate excursion into it. I will say, with David Wood,[3] that the concept of authenticity in Heidegger is ambiguous, and especially so on the question of its positive and negative meanings in relation to how to understand and how to live. The important point for current purposes is that there is a structural connection between the authentic and the inauthentic, and indeed, that for Heidegger, there is always something inauthentic in the authentic. The issue of authenticity at it features in Heidegger is a digression from the central concern here which is to describe the temporality of being in its relation to the temporality of reading. But it is an issue of such importance to the phenomenological approach to temporality that it is difficult to leave it out, particularly when it is developed in such close association with the question of anticipation.

For Heidegger, the priority of the future cannot be understood in terms of the ordinary conception of the future. It is the authentic part of the present: the moment of vision which takes place in the present but looks forward to outcomes, through which Being better understands itself. This 'better understanding' of itself is a project which derives from one of Heidegger's opening characterisations of Dasein, that 'in its very Being . . . Being is an issue for it' (1962: 32). Human being, in other words, is partly defined by thinking about being – '*Understanding of Being is itself a definite characteristic of Dasein's Being*' (his italics, p. 32) – and this understanding is best when it occurs as resolute anticipation. Let us paraphrase this situation in the customary way, namely by using distance as the metaphor which expresses this doubleness of being: that being is always partly at a distance from itself. In the act of reflecting upon itself, it will be reflecting upon the fact that it is, in its nature, self-reflecting. This is what distinguishes human being from the being of rabbits and rocks. As Sartre puts it in *Being and Nothingness*, the thing reflected upon is profoundly affected by the fact that 'the reflective consciousness must be the consciousness reflected on' (1969: 151). Against this rather confusing unity between the subject and the object of reflection, philosophy traditionally resorts to the metaphor of distance. Sometimes this is the spatial distance of the order of 'alongside': 'the turning back of being on itself can only cause the appearance of a *distance* between what turns back and that on which it turns. This turning back upon the self is a wrenching away from self in order to return to it' (his italics, p. 151). The temporal version of this distance is also a wrenching away and a return, that is, a projection forward into the future in order to return to reflect on the self as an object of the quasi-past. This is what Heidegger means when he talks about the future as Being-coming-towards-itself: that the future-oriented project of anticipatory resoluteness creates a split in the self and produces a temporal distance between the reflective consciousness and the consciousness reflected on, a distance which decreases as Dasein tries to catch up with, or actualise, its own projections. One of the things that this metaphor of distance confirms is that some remains of the distinction between subject and object are to be found in the phenomenology of Heidegger and Sartre, since the unity of the reflective consciousness and the consciousness reflected on is inexpressible without this schism and the distance between the two modes of self that are created by it.

Narrative theory has something to learn from Heidegger's and Sartre's rejection of the present as the basis of human being, but it may also have something to teach philosophy when it comes to the issue of distance. Wayne Booth's monumental study of narrative point of view, *The Rhetoric of Fiction*, is the most systematic account of distance in the structure of narrative. For Booth, distance is the framework which gives fictional discourse its layers, and the basis of most of its rhetorical effects. He enumerates various forms of distance which authors establish and abolish at their whim, as well as forms of distance which are adopted by readers of fiction. In the case of authorially controlled distance, he establishes a set of spatial relations in which distance can be controlled: distance between the narrator and the implied author, between narrator and characters, between the narrator and the reader, between the implied author and the reader, the implied author and characters, etc. The nature of the distance that can occur in any of these relations also varies: it may be physical, in the sense that the narrator may describe from a distant point of view, it may be temporal, in the sense of distant retrospect, or it may be moral in the sense that the narrator may judge the moral character of the characters he narrates. In the case of reader-controlled distance, Booth offers a set of resistances which a reader might adopt, normally on the basis of moral difference, in relation to characters, narrators or implied authors which an author may attempt to overcome through his ultimate control of narrative distance, and in this interaction lies the persuasive power of fiction. The control of distance is often divided between author and reader, for example in the case of aesthetic distance, which means on the one hand a kind of critical sophistication adopted by a reader which distances that reader from the involvement which might normally be brought about by the mechanisms of fiction, and on the other, a kind of authorial control which creates such readerly distance, in the manner, perhaps, of Brechtian alienation.

This is an immensely productive analytical framework for Booth and through it he produces highly illuminating readings of Henry James, Jane Austen and James Joyce. If Sartre's concept of distance is that which appears between the reflective consciousness and the consciousness reflected on, Booth's concept seems most germane when addressed to the question of first person narration. Before I discuss the idea of first person narration as self-distance, however, it is worthwhile dwelling on the overall framework for some preliminary types of self-distance which operate slightly less consciously in the system. The very idea of an implied author, which Booth describes as the 'second self' created for the purposes of novelistic communication, provides one type of self-distance which inhabits this analytical system. The idea of 'aesthetic distance' is another example, which Booth holds up as a critical virtue, and which involves a kind of superiority over the common reader which one might associate with academic criticism. He claims, for example, that 'only an immature reader ever identifies with any character, losing all sense of distance and hence all possibility of an artistic experience' (1961: 200). The proximity of identification is uncritical in contrast to the distance of artistic experience, and this establishes an interesting split in the act of reading. It suggests a division in being according to which the aesthetically distanced reader both reads and is conscious of reading, both a reader and a witness of the reading process, where what is witnessed (naïve reading) is disowned. Or perhaps not. Perhaps the naïve reading is never actually witnessed by the aesthetically distanced one but imagined as the act of another. In which case we are left with a different kind of split, or self-distance. Sartre notes that

> Reflection as witness can have its being as witness only in and through the appearance; that is, it is profoundly affected in its being by its reflectivity and consequently can never achieve the Selbstandigkeit (self-standingness) at which it aims. (1969: 152)

This means that the naïve reading knows itself observed, and therefore never occurs as such, since it is already altered by this knowing. I would suggest that we all know this problem whenever we drift into the fantasy that our innermost thoughts are being observed, by God, a law court or a friend, only to realise that the content of those thoughts is therefore the fantasy of such an inspection itself.

This helps to highlight the importance of temporal distance in reflection and self-narration. No difficulty is presented to the idea of reflection when the subject and object of reflection are separated in time, but when they coincide, a logical regress is produced which makes it impossible to reflect on anything except reflection itself. Sartre does not quite say this, and this is where I believe the philosophy of reflection may have something to learn from the theory of narrative. When the reflected and the reflective coincide, Sartre tends to describe them as if they are both together and separate: 'its meaning as reflected-on is inseparable from the reflective and exists over there at a distance from itself in the consciousness which reflects it' (1969: 152). This is the spatial distance of 'over there' rather than the temporal distance of 'back then' about which narrative knows so much. Phenomenology has a highly developed sense of the future when it comes to the imbrication of presence with future projections, but a less developed sense of the future projection as a manner in which distance between the subject and object of reflection can be produced. This is certainly not to say that philosophy in general has been unaware of the paradoxes of reflection or of self-referentiality: it could be argued that this awareness is what philosophy *is* above all else. But there is an interesting little kingdom of expertise on this subject, which foregrounds the role of narrative consciousness in the production of temporal distance between the self as the reflected-on and as reflective consciousness, and which is found in the analysis of self-narration in narratology.

The fundamental problem of phenomenology is a question of immanence: how can a consciousness explain something which it cannot stand outside? This is what is expressed by Sartre's paradoxical formula which envisages the reflective and the reflected as simultaneously unified and separated, or singular and double. One might say that there is a logical problem that emerges whenever the subject and the object merge as they do in the act of self-reflection. Nor is this a problem confined to the issue of 'consciousness': it operates in any situation which involves self-reference. The liar paradox is a good example of the havoc that self-referentiality produces in logical terms. If I say that I am lying, it becomes impossible to judge the truth of what I am saying. If I am indeed lying then what I say is not true, in which case I cannot be telling the truth that I am lying, and so I must be telling the truth. This logical havoc is produced by the co-incidence of the statement and what it refers to in time. It is the kind of problem that arises in cases of self-referentiality, and can be easily solved by the introduction of some kind of separation between the saying and the said. If I claim, for example, that 'all generalisations are false', the same thing happens because, as a generalisation, the statement is included in the set of statements it judges. The statement 'all generalisations are false, except this one' is not logically contradictory in the same way – does not have the value of true and false – because the statement exempts itself from the set of its referents. This exemption is a kind of distance between the subject and the object of a statement, and one kind of distance that can be deployed in this way is temporal distance. If I say that 'I used to be a liar', no problem arises. The statement is still self-referential, but the change of tense produces distance between the subject and the object of the statement.

The study of narrative has much to learn from the philosophy of time, but this is one of the places where the direction of teaching is the other way around. It is true that symbolic logic has made major advances into the role of tense in valid argument forms in recent decades, but the more thorough expertise in the analysis of the temporal distance involved in a statement such as 'I used to be a liar', seems to me to lie with narratology, especially as it has accounted for the subtleties of unreliable narration. Again Booth is a pioneer here, and his framework of the varieties of distance allows an analysis which sees a statement such as 'I used to be a liar' as two different forms of distance at the same time: it contains the temporal distance of tense, but also moral distance, the self-distance of moral judgement. One of the interesting things about Booth's analysis of unreliable narration is that it demonstrates the distance between a narrator and a reader in circumstances in which the reliability of that narrator has come into question: when a narrator tries to mislead, or simply does not know the truth. But this is not exactly the situation here. What is perhaps less noticeable about the tensed statement 'I used to be a liar' is that it constructs a contrast between the 'I' of the time of narration and the 'I' of narrated time along the lines that the former is truthful and the latter dishonest. This is a common paradigm for narrative discourse in general, and narrative fiction in particular. It is the paradigm of the confession, in which a reformed narrator looks back on what a sinner he or she used to be. Such narratives must involve the moral self-distance of the confessor, as exemplified by Hogg's Robert Wringham in *The Private Memoirs and Confessions of a Justified Sinner*:

> As I am writing only from recollection, so I remember of nothing farther in these early days, in the least worthy of being recorded. That I was a great and repentant sinner, I confess. But still I had hopes of forgiveness, because I never sinned from principle, but accident; and then I always *tried* to repent of these sins by the slump, for individually it was impossible; and though not always successful in my endeavours, I could not help that; the grace of repentance being withheld from me, I regarded myself as in no way accountable for the failure. (1981: 113)

The moral distance between the narrator and the narrated here is permitted by the temporal distance between the recollection and the recollected, and it works in two ways. It is both the recounting of sin, and the recounting of the justification of sin so that the distance is directed towards events and the mind that accounted for them. It is not only that I used to sin, Wringham tells us, but that I used to deceive myself as to the sinfulness of my sins. Just as the liar paradox establishes a moral contrast between the liar of the past and the present truth-teller, so the confession contrasts the moral personality or the narrator with that of the narrated, as reliable narration of a former unreliability, or the truth about lies.

The most interesting aspect of confessional narratives in my view is that they almost always entail a steady decrease in temporal distance between the narrator and the narrated, and this must necessarily entail the erosion of the moral distance between the confessor and the confessed. When exactly did the liar of the past transform into the honest narrator of the present? Self-distance must end in self-presence as the events of a life catch up with the moment of telling it, and somewhere in this narrative, the moral transformation of the narrator is required in order to protect the discourse itself from the moral failings, such as lying, which it narrates. In Wringham's case the deceit simply doesn't stop, and we witness him lying right up to the end of his narrative. Lying in fact becomes the closing theme of the novel, not only because Wringham continues to narrate his own lies as he runs from the law (he tells the guests in a hotel that he is a poor theology student from Oxford), but because the ensuing question about the reliability of the memoir then migrates metaleptically to the editor's narrative which closes the novel: the manuscript 'bears the stamp of authenticity in every line', and yet 'God knows! Hogg has imposed as ingenious lies on the public ere now' (1969: 245–6). There is a kind of crisis that approaches in confessional narrative as the subject and the object of narration threaten to coincide. Perhaps the most comical example of this is Dr Jekyll's confession in Stevenson's *Dr Jekyll and Mr Hyde*, where the moral narrator and his immoral alter ego literally cannot coincide because they are separately embodied: they are the personifications of the schism of the subject and object of confession.[4]

The most telling example of the confessional narrative in this respect is Saint Augustine's *Confessions*. This is a text well known for its foundational importance in the philosophy of time, but the lesson it teaches about time is not often understood in the context of the crisis that occurs in confessional narrative structure.[5] As for Hogg, the issue of the unreliability of distant recall is prominent in the early stages of Augustine's confession, but in a ludicrously exaggerated form, as the narrator attempts to confess the sins he committed when he was a baby. He cannot remember these sins, but he knows he must have committed them, since other babies do. The sins are heinous indeed:

> So I would toss my arms and legs about and make noises, hoping that such few signs as I could make would show my meaning . . . and if my wishes were not carried out . . . I would get cross with my elders . . . and I would take revenge by bursting into tears. (1961: 25–6).

There is a danger that we start to read this moral supererogation as spoofery, as ironic confession, so unwarranted is the self-admonishment for these reconstructed sins, and yet there is something comically convincing about the tone of questioning that pervades his account of babyhood, that 'if babies are innocent, it is not for lack of will to do harm, but for lack of strength' (28). And yet this is anything but irony, and the progress of the confession assures us that the sins that we commit as babies, of which we have no memory, are no different from the sins that we remember, but which were committed in a state of ignorance of the truth, or of distance from God. The confession is in its nature a recollection of a state of ignorance, and this means that it is not a recollection at all, since you cannot remember what you did not know. The recognition of ignorance comes later, and in the form of a realisation of ignorance which accompanies the narration of events, so that the moral distance between the narrator and the narrated becomes a kind of announcement, paradoxically, of the unreliability of the narrator, despite his location after the enlightenment in the domain of truth. There is no logical difference then between the narrator who recalls the sins he cannot remember as a baby, and one who writes 'I knew nothing of this at the time. I was quite unconscious of it, quite blind to it, although it stared me in the face' (33). Sentences such as this pervade Augustine's recollections, and remind us of the future, or the future of confession in psychoanalysis. In the Freudian tradition, psychoanalysis operates on the assumption that mental disturbance is a state of self-ignorance to be overcome in the moment of narration by self-knowledge. The past, in other words was a lie, and the present is the cure in the form of truthful, reliable self-narration. But in the act of self-narration, the unreliability of the narrator merely takes a new form, remembering the past not as it was, but in the light of the present. In order to tell the truth about a lie, one must tell a lie about the truth, both of which, as every philosopher knows, result in a lie.

In Book X of *Confessions*, the question of memory, of its reliability as an account of the past, comes to the fore. It is in fact an essential step-ping-stone in the narrowing gap between the narrator and his creator, or between falsehood and truth. To find God, we must go beyond the senses, and towards those faculties not shared by horses and mules, which comprise the soul. Here the narrative recedes to give way to a philosophical contemplation, and the actions of remembering and forgetting which have constituted the narrative become objects of direct reflection:

> I can mention forgetfulness and recognize what the word means, but how can I recognize the thing itself unless I remember it? I am not speaking of the sound of the word but of the thing which it signifies. If I had forgotten the thing itself, I should be utterly unable to recognize what the sound implied. When I remember memory, my memory is present to itself by its own power; but when I remember forgetfulness, two things are present, memory, by which I remember it, and forgetfulness, which is what I remember. Yet what is forgetfulness but absence of memory? When it is present, I cannot remember. Then how can it be present in such a way that I can remember it? If it is true that what we remember we retain in our memory, and if it is also true that unless we remembered forgetfulness, we could not possibly recognize the meaning of the word when we heard it, then it is true that forgetfulness is retained in the memory. It follows that the very thing which by its presence causes us to forget must be present if we are to remember it. Are we to understand from this that, when we remember it, it is not itself present in the memory, but is only there by means if its image? For if forgetfulness were itself present, would not its effect be to make us forget, not to remember? (1961: 222)

The answer to this looks straightforward. I can remember forgetting a meeting yesterday, therefore it is perfectly possible to remember forgetting. But am I really remembering what it was like to forget, in the sense of making it present? After all, forgetting the meeting yesterday was very much like not having one at all, in fact it felt exactly the same as not forgetting anything. To remember it as forgetting is to fail to remember it as it was, since it only becomes forgetting after I have remembered the meeting. The simple answer to the question then, that remembering forgetting is unproblematic, takes it for granted that memory entails the temporal distance between the self as the object and as the subject of narration. We might say that it is implicit in the words 'memory' and 'remember' that the kind of presence, understood as temporal co-incidence, on which Augustine's aporia is founded, is banished, so that temporal distance is the very basis of their intelligibility. But to submit to this pragmatic solution is to allow the unexamined notions of 'remembering' and 'forgetting' the power to lie undetected. We might agree here with Heidegger that the idea of retention as a 'making present' of the past is human temporality operating in its most inauthentic mode, or with Deleuze in *Difference and Repetition* when he argues that it is 'futile to try to reconstitute the past from the presents between which it is trapped, either the present which it was or the one in relation to which it is now past' (1994: 81). Remembering is never real, in the sense of making present again the former present of the past. In the act of remembering, we transform the former present, and this is particularly clear in the memory of forgetting, which is identified as forgetting only by becoming what it was not. The temporal self-distance of retrospect is a lie which reveals the truth, and this renders the truth a matter of temporality rather than simple presence.

The nature of the confessional narrative is to offer an unfolding allegory of the temporality of all language. It presents an example of the collapse of temporal distance in the act of self-narration. As the self of the past catches up with the self of the present, and as narrated time threatens to coincide with the time of the narrative, a crisis beckons. In the case of memory, this crisis would happen regardless of the conspiracy of moral and temporal distance of confession. When narrated time catches up with the time of the narrative, there is nothing left to remember but memory itself, and nothing left to write about but the act of writing. And this is exactly what happens in *Confessions*. Whereas Dr Jekyll's moment of co-incidence with himself is death and silence, since Hyde kills him, Augustine's involves a frantic philosophical conversation with God before the silence. When he no longer has any past to narrate, the narration turns to consider itself and the very temporal problems that narrative self-reflection raises. Commentators often speak, as Kermode does, of the 'great eleventh chapter of Augustine's *Confessions*' (1966: 53) as if it were a detachable tract on the nature of time. But just as Book

X is a reflection on the issues of forgetting that begin in babyhood, and represent a response to the problem of what to do when remembered events coincide with the act of remembering, so too, Book XI reflects on the problem of presence towards which the narrative is moving from its beginnings. The quest for truth is expressed from the start in terms of distance:

> How long it was before I learned that you were my true joy! You were silent then, and I went on my way, farther and farther from you, proud in my distress and restless in fatigue, sowing more and more seeds whose only crop was grief. (1961: 44)

There are three types of distance that cooperate here and throughout the narrative. The first is distance from God, the second is distance from truth and the third is temporal distance. The story is told in a proleptic mode, in the sense that it anticipates the time of the narrative at every stage, the eventual reform, the proximity to God and to the truth which lie in wait, and the moral progress entailed in this diminishing distance is itself a guarantee of the reliability of the narrator. The young Augustine is not only a thief and a fornicator, he is a self-deluding liar: 'Many and many a time I lied to my tutor, my masters, and my parents, and deceived them because I wanted to play games or watch some futile show or was impatient to imitate what I saw on stage' (1961: 39). For us to trust him as a narrator, therefore, we need to know that a transformation has occurred which distances him from this past characterised as ignorance and falsehood. The milestones on this quest are unmistakable partly because the idea of distance is a constant metaphor, and one which combines with the conventional Christian tropology of the voice. As above, distance is silence, or the absence of conversation, while proximity is marked by the approach of God's speech. We know that this speech is coming because it is anticipated, again in the mode of Prolepsis 2, which travels forward to the time locus of the narrator: 'as I now know since you have spoken to me.' (1961: 61). When the voice is first heard, it is at a distance – 'And, far off, I hear your voice saying I am the God who IS'[6] (147) – and in the later stages has come so close as to be within, in the heart and soul of the confessor.

A complex self-commentary unfolds with this diminishing distance between falsehood and truth which concerns the nature of philosophy itself. As the confession proceeds, there is a clear shift away from autobiographical narration and a clear increase in philosophical speculation. I have already said that this is one way of dealing with the problem of running out of story to tell, since all that is left to narrate is narration itself. Book XI therefore takes the present as its subject, and not only what is happening now, but the idea of the present. Just as Book X leaves the acts of remembering and forgetting behind in favour of a reflection on remembering and forgetting as abstract philosophical topics, so too Book XI turns its attention from the past to the nature of time in general terms. This is a paradigmatic literary structure which is found in diaries which turn to contemplate the nature of diary-keeping, and of course Proust's discussion of the shape of time in Book VI of *In Search of Lost Time*. But philosophy is not just an activity which Augustine turns to at the end of *Confessions*, it is also a prominent topic of the narration which precedes the more philosophical books. Philosophy is one of the forces that brings the confessor's reform about, acting as a kind of middle ground between rhetoric and the word of God. As a sinner, Augustine is a teacher of literature, and when he emerges from his filthy cauldron of lust at the start of Book III, it is through a rumination on the evils of vicarious experience, in the form of literature and drama, and in particular the evils of pitying those who suffer on stage. The self-commentary here is inevitable, not only because we are in the midst of a vicarious experience of Saint Augustine's own suffering (though no doubt finding Augustine the Sinner infinitely more interesting than Augustine the Saint) but also because it incorporates into his own language and discourse an explicit reflection on language and discourse. The love of literature is, in retrospect, clearly part of his moral turpitude, as is his interest in rhetoric, and Augustine constantly contrasts both with truth, yet it is through the study of rhetoric, and the sense of superiority and conceit which accompanied his success in it, that he came upon philosophy:

> The prescribed course of study brought me to the work of Cicero, whose writing nearly everyone admires, if not the spirit of it. The title of the book is *Hortensius* and it recommends the reader to study philosophy. It altered my outlook on life. It changed my prayers to you, O Lord, and provided me with new hopes and aspirations. All my empty dreams suddenly lost their charm and my heart began to throb with a bewildering passion for the wisdom of eternal truth. I began to climb out of the depths to which I had sunk, in order to return to you. For I did not use the book to sharpen my tongue. It was not the style of it but the contents which won me over. (1961: 58–9)

Though full of lies, literature led him to the vanity of rhetoric, which presented him with philosophy, which satisfied a love of wisdom and truth and led him closer to God. As such, his narrative enacts the story it tells, since it not only describes the conversion in these terms, but also gradually abandons narrative in favour of philosophy. The confession narrates a whole set of transitions which it also enacts in its own style and structure, from distance to proximity, from youth to wisdom, from falsity to truth, from literature to philosophy and from devilry to God, and in this way it holds the past at bay, and prevents the moral unreliability of the past from contaminating the truth of the present.

But it is very difficult to see this transition as a success, or indeed to see the philosophy of time presented in Book XI as anything other than a subversion of this separation of lies from truth. From the very moment that Augustine announces the discovery of philosophy, he also warns against the dangers of philosophy, and of its potential to deceive and mislead:

> There are people for whom philosophy is a means of misleading others, for they misuse its great name, its attractions, and its integrity to give colour and gloss to their own errors. Most of these so-called philosophers who lived in Cicero's time and before are noted in the book. He shows them up in their true colours and makes quite clear how wholesome is the admonition which the Holy Spirit gives in the words of your good and true servant, Paul: *Take care not to let anyone cheat you with his philosophizings, with empty fantasies drawn from human tradition, from worldly principles; they were never Christ's teaching.* (59)

Augustine's training in rhetoric was clearly not wasted, and we see him here excelling in the mode of rhetorical prolepsis, in anticipation of an argument against the truth-telling powers of philosophy. At the moment of declaring that he has moved on from the trickery of rhetoric to the truth of philosophy, he rolls out the oldest trick in the rhetorical handbook, namely the preclusion of an objection through its anticipation. This moment in Book III bears a very complex relationship with the philosophisings of Book XI. If it succeeds as prolepsis, it will preclude the objection to philosophy, and in so doing affirm the trickery of rhetoric against which the truth of philosophy is defined. If on the other hand it fails, it will install in the reader exactly the suspicion that it aims to preclude: the suspicion that philosophers might be cheating us. Either way, the prolepsis contaminates the truth to come with the falsity which it aims to leave behind, to relegate to the past. Augustine is merely repeating the trick played upon him by Cicero, the great master of prolepsis, in order to convince his readers of the truth of his own claim that the philosophers of the past are liars, and so that they belong with his own youthful personality on the other side of the moral contrast of the confession to his own narrative present. There is internal anticipation here, of the philosophy to come, and there is external anticipation, which works on the objections of the reader, and which reveals the fiction of a private conversation with God in its own true rhetorical colours.

How does this rhetorical and narratological reading affect the content of what Augustine argues about time in Book XI? One answer to this has already been offered. Book XI may have been taken by philosophers as a detachable tract about time, but it is also a tract embedded in the narrative structure of a self-reflection, and more specifically, in the logical problems of truth and falsity faced by self-referential discourses. It would be melodramatic to say that Book XI is not about time, but about narrative, and perhaps more accurate to claim that it is incapable of holding these two subjects apart. The distance between time and narrative cannot be maintained, because the philosophical discussion erupts as a necessary reflection on the temporal crisis which occurs when a dishonest past catches up with the moment of sincere narration which seeks to exclude it. But this is not the end of the story. In the analysis above it is clear that the confession depends on the separation of lies from truth, and therefore on the temporal distance that the narrative provides as a mechanism. Yet the contribution which Book XI has made to the philosophy of time is exactly the opposite of this, insofar as it places in question the very possibility of separation on which the narrative depends.

The argument of Book XI is well known: time thought of as a series of 'nows' is incoherent, in that it seems to suggest that nothing has any existence. The past does not exist, because it is by definition what used to exist, and the future does not exist yet. Yet the present also cannot exist because it has no duration: as soon as it does have duration it can be divided into future and past segments, and in the process rules itself out of existence again. The solution to this is to endow past, present and future with existence by translating them into memory, direct perception and expectation, since these correspond to three things that clearly do have existence: the present of past things, the present of present things and the present of future things. The example through which this is argued is the perception of sunrise:

> Suppose that I am watching the break of day. I predict that the sun is about to rise. What I see is present but what I foretell is future. I do not mean that the sun is future, for it already exists, but that its rise is future, because it has not yet happened. But I could not foretell the sunrise unless I had a picture of it in my mind., just I have at this moment while I am speaking about it. Yet the dawn, which I see in the sky, is not the sunrise, which is future. The future, then, is not yet; it is not at all, it cannot possibly be seen. But it can be foretold from things which are present, because they exist now and can therefore be seen. (268)

In this moment before sunrise, it is claimed, something is present to the eye, and that something contains within it traces of what has been and what is to come. This is fundamentally the phenomenological view of time that we find in Husserl, where the present is a crossed structure of protentions and retentions, and in Heidegger's unity of ecstases. But Heidegger, as we have seen, rejects presence as the foundation of existence, and the reasons for this show up very clearly in the relation between Augustine's argument and his example. First he says that presence has no existence because it has no duration, then that presence can be divided into three. This is normally taken not as a contradiction, but as a moment of genius which compensates for the lack of extension of the present with the distension of presence in the mind. In other words, it is not that the present doesn't exist, but that it exists in a particular way to the mind, as a crossed structure of protentions and retentions. The past and the future are therefore merely aspects of the present, or rather that they only have existence for humans as presence, in the present. What then is the Other of time? For Augustine it is God, who is outside time, in eternity. Yet eternity itself is 'a never-ending present'. Despite the lack of extension of the present, it would appear that for both the human and the divine mind, the present is all we have, and that the distension of past, present and future in the human mind creates a kind of fragment of that complete unity, the never-ending present, apprehended by God.

The past, according to this scheme, exists for the human mind only as the present of the past. Like Heidegger, Augustine offers an account of the experience of time as an ineluctable unity, and one which differs from the ordinary conception of time. But whereas Heidegger rigorously substitutes the familiar and commonsensical words (past, present and future) with new terms and phrases, Augustine is content to continue with the old ones despite their potentially misleading effect:

> By all means, then, let us speak of three times, past, present and future. Incorrect though it is, let us comply with usage. I shall not object or argue, nor shall I rebuke anyone who speaks in these terms, provided that he understand what he is saying and does not imagine that the future or the past exists now. Our use of words is generally inaccurate and seldom completely correct, but our meaning is recognized none the less. (1961: 269)

The disarming candour with which he warned against the dangers of philosophy is repeated here in relation to language more generally, in the warning that words themselves are not accurate, and particularly that the words 'past', 'present' and 'future' do not mean what they say. The relationship between confession and philosophising reaches a new level of tension here. It is not only that the narrative structure of the confession seems to depend upon the temporal separation of the narrator and the narrated, or Augustine past and present, it is also that the very words, and indeed tenses, of the narrative are rooted in a philosophy of time which the philosophical reflections reject. Put at its most simple, the features of discourse which mark its retrospect, such as past tenses and temporal locators such as 'once' and 'then' are misleading us into thinking that the past is before us, when in fact only the present is present. The word 'past' is a lie because it disguises the presence of the present. This is a confession that knows that it cannot deliver the truth about time, because that truth is outside of human time, in the eternity experienced by God. The contrast that Augustine develops between time and eternity therefore works to establish that time itself is a lie.

On one hand *Confessions* seems to depend upon the separability, or the temporal distance, which is permitted by the separation of past, present and future. On the other hand, the narration seems not only to enact, but to state explicitly, that this temporal separability is impossible. This paradox is not as much of a calamity, or even a logical inconsistency, as it may appear. If the threefold present is inescapable for the human mind, we are merely saying that the temporal distance that separates the past from the present, and which permits the moral self-judgement of confession is immanent in the present. The paradox then is that this temporal distance is not actually temporally distant, and indeed that no temporal distance can ever really exist for the human mind, since presence is all that there is. But in the terms of Augustine's own argument, there is no presence either, since as soon as there is presence, in the sense that presence has duration, there is only absence in the form of the past and the future. As Heidegger well knew, presence cannot function as the principle that unifies present, past and future, and it is obvious that Augustine's argument is simply contradictory. It argues first that the present has no extension, and then that it is distended in the human mind; but it is illogical that something which has no extension can be distended, since the condition of lacking extension is the condition of not being distended.

As David Wood remarks in his discussion of Heidegger,[7] it is difficult to make sense of any purely phenomenological account of time, that is of the threefold present, or of the unity of the ecstases, without reference to an external, cosmological or ordinary conception of time. How, asks Ricoeur, can we make sense of the threefold present, or of the distension of the present in the mind, without reference to an objective and cosmological sense of the past, present and future? The very meanings of 'memory', 'direct experience' and 'expectation' are dependent on the concepts of the past, present and future. It would seem that what happens in the account of temporality offered by both Augustine and Heidegger is that the ordinary conception of time as a series of nows, with the past behind us and the future before us, is merely relocated within consciousness, so that the idea of time as a product of the mind is merely an immanent repetition of the ordinary conception of time. Augustine's relocation of the past, the present and the future is of course based on the argument that neither the past and future, nor the present can exist, in the sense of being present to consciousness. But this is an entirely circular argument: it begins from the presupposition that existence is presence to consciousness, and proceeds to demonstrate that presence is never present to consciousness, only to conclude that nothing exists. The argument that the lack of extension of the present is compensated for by the distension of the threefold present by the mind is nothing more than a bid to rescue the situation from the abyss of nonexistence by resurrecting the notion of presence, which reappears without justification as the basis on which things exist in the mind. In other words the view of time as the threefold present can only be half of the picture, and though the human mind can have no direct access to the other half, that is to the direct perception of past and future in their entirety, the intuition of the past and the future is necessary to the present, and to the conception of the threefold present. The paradox of temporal distance then is merely the recognition that an account of the inseparability of past, present and future in the mind depends upon their separation in the ordinary, or metaphysical, conception of time, and in reverse, that the metaphysical conception of time cannot deny the inseparability of past, present and future in consciousness.

But is consciousness the right frame of reference here? Many parts of Augustine's argument offer a notion of presence to the mind as the foundation for being and time, but when we move forwards in the history of philosophy, there is a discernible tendency to displace the notion of consciousness with the category of language itself, or to shift from the analysis of the mind to an analysis of textuality. The notion of narrative consciousness is itself something of a conflation of the externality of writing and the internality of consciousness, and it is to this monistic universe, to this rebellion against the idea of consciousness itself that a theory aiming to encompass the written text and a mode of being under the rubric of narrative must turn.

Notes

1. For a discussion of authentic ways of relating to past, present and future, see David Wood 2001: 225–6.
2. For good measure, the critique of this passage might also include the charge of vagueness, in the form of the weak logical relation 'in terms of': 'temporality temporalizes itself in terms of the authentic future'. There is also a trace of the common charge against Heidegger's style, namely that it is dominated

by polyptoton, or the use of the same word stem in a multitude of forms. In this case the term 'futurally', which has marked the difference between temporality and time throughout the discussion, is used to underpin the priority of the future in authentic temporality, and so partakes of the tautology discussed above.

3. See David Wood 2001: 225–6. The centre of Wood's case is that, in the idea of authenticity, Heidegger may have transformed a positive into a negative value, and that authentic understanding may be more properly understood as a *not knowing*. The sense of ambiguity is compounded in my view by a more fundamental one between description and evaluation in themselves: between the project which aims to describe human Being, and that which aims to tell humans how to act.

4. For a full reading of *Dr Jekyll and Mr Hyde* and the crisis involved in the narrowing of temporal distance, see Mark Currie 1998, pp. 117–34.

5. Genevieve Lloyd's excellent reading of *Confessions* in Chapter 1 of *Being in Time* is perhaps an exception. The emphasis of this reading is not on the narrowing moral and temporal gap between narrated time and the time of the narrative, but its central conviction is that it must be understood in terms of its narrative structure.

6. The utterance is a citation from Exodus 3:14.

7. David Wood 2001: 247–9.

Chapter 5

Inner and Outer Time

Time is a river which sweeps me along, but I am the river.
(Borges 1964: 187)

The previous chapters open a set of questions about the relationship between time and self-consciousness, an axis which has received too little attention within literary studies.[1] This neglect is all the more surprising since the idea of self-consciousness itself has played such a central role in the characterisation not only of contemporary fiction but of the more general social and discursive condition of the contemporary world. In prolepsis, we find on one hand a kind of temporal self-distance – a form of reflection which involves looking back on the present, from one's own point of view or that of another – and on the other hand a kind of reversed causation, in which this future retrospect causes the event it looks back on. But can this really be thought of as reversed causation or backwards time? The purpose of this chapter is to explore this question alongside a consideration of the relationship between time, consciousness and self-consciousness.

To begin, we might revisit the question of Derridean supplementarity, formulated in *Speech and Phenomena* as a temporal structure in which 'a possibility produces that to which it is said to be added on' and which in *Archive Fever* takes the form 'the archive produces the event as much as it records it'. In both cases, the word 'produces' indicates causality, so that the later possibility or the recording archive are assigned the status of cause in spite of their posteriority. And yet this posterior cause need not be viewed with any real surprise, since the posteriority of the cause is imagined and not real: it is a protention or anticipation of the future that causes the event, and not any reversal of the expansion of the universe. Hence, the case of an archive producing the news event cannot be seen as the future causing the present, but only as a possibility – a possible or envisaged future – which takes place in the present as a kind of psychological cause. This kind of structure of supplementarity is in fact no more surprising than the idea of an intention, a fear or a hope as the motivating force of an action. There are cases, in Derrida, where the claim seems to be a little stronger or more surprising than this, such as the much vaunted argument that writing precedes speech. But again that argument in *Of Grammatology* does not claim the objective posteriority of speech to writing, and amounts to little more than an admission that speech precedes writing coupled to a claim that, just because it precedes it in clock time, it ought not to be accorded any conceptual priority. In the case of speech and writing, the possibility which produces that to which it is said to be added on, the possibility of writing, is not some psychologically envisaged future, but rather a logical possibility, which, on analysis, turns out to display all the essential conditions upon which significance depends. Again, it would be a mistake to think that the second law of thermodynamics was in any way at stake in this. We might say, as we did in the previous chapter, that what is really at stake here is phenomenological rather than cosmological time, or a certain slippage between the two which gives deconstruction some of its more melodramatic formulations. We might say, with Ricoeur, that it is the very nature of narrative, especially in its fictional form, to explore the interaction of phenomenological and cosmological time, and therefore between Husserlian protentions and actual futures.

There are many simple ways of illustrating the difference between subjective and objective time. The first is the example of the person who sits on a drawing pin, and who jumps up in response to a sudden jab of pain.[2] In phenomenological terms, the sequence of this experience is 'pain' followed by 'pin', in the sense that the pain comes first and the discovery of the pin follows from it. But this is clearly not the same as saying that the pain caused the pin, and the rational response to this experience is to reorder the experiential sequence pain/pin into a causal one – pin/pain. Interestingly, when Jonathan Culler uses this example in *On Deconstruction*, he does so in order to claim that causation itself is at stake in the disjunction between the temporal sequence of the experience and that of the story we tell about it, and in order to demonstrate that the deconstruction of causation relies on the notion of cause: 'the experience of pain, it is claimed, causes us to discover the pin and thus causes the production of a cause' (1983: 87). Ricoeur, on the other hand, would view narrative as a place in which the objective and subjective aspects of this situation might be reconciled with each other, so that narrative is seen as a place in which the tension between the two sequences, and therefore the interaction of a subject with the cosmos, can be most adequately explored. The first view seems to suggest that scientific causality is mere storytelling, while the second seems to view the two models of temporality as a kind of aporia for which narrative offers a potential resolution. Another way of approaching this problem is through the idea of psychological duration. A lecture which lasts for one hour may seem to take much longer if it fails to interest a particular member of the audience: in psychological time there is a sense of greater duration which is contradicted by the clock. Just as the pin/pain example tends to view the experiential sequence as an illusion and the causal sequence as reality, so too in the example of psychological duration, the clock is the measurement of real time whereas the mind is the place of illusion and appearance. This distinction places us in the middle of a set of problems well known in philosophy and the philosophy of science about the nature of reason. We might begin with Kant's *Critique of Pure Reason*, which cannot countenance the idea that we have access to things in themselves, or *noumena*, and assembles its account of speculative reason on the premise that we can deal only with things as they appear to the senses, or *phenomena*. In terms of the nature of time, we must ask how the notion of scientific causality has acquired the status of a *noumenology* of time, while philosophy has confined itself to a *phenomenology* of time, as if science deals with the universe and philosophy with the mind. A reading of Stephen Hawking's *A Brief History of Time* suggests that this division of labour is predicated on complete disinterest in, and perhaps an irrational fear of, the philosophy of time, but we ought not to judge theoretical physics as a whole in this way. Nor would we want to uphold the oppositions of subjective and objective time, psychological and clock time, or phenomenological and cosmological time too rigidly after Einstein.

It is clear that Derridean supplementarity has its roots in phenomenology, but it may also have more in common with the Modernist novel than it does with Husserl and Heidegger. Derrida's *différance* emerges from the view borrowed from Husserl of the present as a crossed structure of protentions and retentions, the view that the present is always divided between the past and the future, even in its apparently most extreme forms, such as the moment of an origin. We might link this idea with the structuralist conception of the sign, which proposes that the content of a sign is not only enabled by but actually constituted by its relations with other signs with which it forms a system. The present, like meaning in general, and for Derrida they amount to the same thing, is nothing in itself, but is actually constituted by its relations to past and future. The value here of the analogy with the linguistic sign is that it begins to point to the way that supplementarity, for all its phenomenological rooting, should not be thought as a mere preference for the mind over the world. It is exactly the impossibility of separating the mind from the world, or language from the world, that gives supplementarity its character as a way of thinking about phenomenological and cosmological time together. From this point of view, Derrida and Ricoeur seem close together on the question of the reality of time, and perhaps this makes some sense of the claim that Derrida's approach is as close to the Modernist novel as to philosophical phenomenology: both may view narrative fiction as a kind of discourse in which the objective and subjective dimensions of time can find their most unified treatments. This is a proposition that I will return to throughout the study. For the moment it is worth highlighting its consequences for the idea incumbent on the logic of supplementarity that an effect might be anterior to a cause.

Time cannot go backwards. If the logic of supplementarity claims otherwise it cannot be saying anything meaningful about the cosmos or the clock. Protentions must not be confused with actual futures. Protentions are mere mental orientations towards the future, and it is banal to say that they produce events in the present. The forward direction of time is enshrined in the second law of thermodynamics, which states that time is asymmetrical because heat will flow from a warmer region to a cooler one but not vice versa. Light travels away from its sources and not towards them. The one-directionality of time is part of the physical fact of an expanding universe. And none of us is getting any younger. How feeble the interventions of the postmodern novelist, the poststructuralist philosopher and the cultural theorist appear in the face of these brute realities.

To continue for a moment with this blatantly rhetorical prolepsis, the only purpose of which can be to preclude the objections it assembles, even though to do so I might have to reverse the expansion of the universe, it may be worth identifying some further propositions about time which for all their influence in contemporary thought, appear feeble in their response to the authority of cosmological time. It is apparently a widely held view, for example, that the one-directional linearity of time is placed in question by the narrative of *Mrs Dalloway* since the order of narrated events follows the digressions of Clarissa's interiority in contrast to the clock time which chimes throughout the day. This can only be viewed as a misunderstanding. Even in the case of a fictional narrative dominated by what Genette calls anachronies, it would be difficult to claim that the forward movement of time was in any way in question. Genette simply refers us in such cases to the discrepancy between story order and text order, or the way that events are assumed to have occurred chronologically and the order in which they are presented in the text.

Mrs Dalloway, however, is not anachronous in this way. It adheres to a strict linearity in its narration of Clarissa's thoughts and those of other characters, and therefore demonstrates one of the problems outlined in the previous chapter: that when analepsis functions in the mode of memory, it needn't be viewed as an anachrony at all, since the memory itself is an event in the fictional present. The more sophisticated version of the claim for the statement that *Mrs Dalloway* makes about time is that it is a detailed examination of the way that we experience time, and since our experience of a phenomenon is the only possible access we can have to it, we must view time not in terms of the clock but as a combination of phenomenological experience and cosmological laws. From this point of view, the novel is a scaled up version of the pin/pain problem and presents the issue of the authority of objective time in relation to the experience of time as it takes place in the minds of several characters. This is the basis of Ricoeur's claim for the novel: that the complex embedded structure of memory, and of the reverberation of one character's solitary experience within another solitary experience produces a kind of network of temporal experience. This network, in turn, 'confronts' what he calls monumental time, the audible experience of which is the striking of clocks throughout the narrative. This more complex point is part of Ricoeur's larger exploration of narrative and its dealings with the aporias of cosmological and phenomenological time. But to claim as Ricoeur does that these aspects of time must be thought about in combination is not to offer any challenge to the asymmetry or the one-directionality of time. The subjective and the objective aspects of time represented in this, and indeed any other novel, may in some ways seem incompatible or, with Ricoeur, aporetic, but not in such a way that the forward direction of time is placed in question. In phenomenological terms, in which the present is a crossed structure of protentions and retentions, there is no limit to the potential anachronies of a sequence of experiences, but they are only anachronous in relation to an objective or external conception of time. What we have to move away from, as Ricoeur constantly reminds us, is a simplistic opposition between clock time and internal time. Nor should we, as I suggested above, view cosmological time as a kind of noumenon which lies outside our experience of it. It is a mistake to align phenomenological time with the life of the mind and cosmological time with the outside world. If, with Hegel in *Phenomenology of Spirit*, we abandon the idea of the noumenon, of things in themselves to which we have no access, on the grounds that we have no access to them, we are left with a kind of cosmological time conceived and perceived from within human experience and so the mind. From this point of view, the aporia of cosmological and phenomenological time is not the same thing as the difference between actual time and the experience of time. Properly speaking, both cosmological and phenomenological time are experiences which are available to the consciousness. What Ricoeur shows so well is that these two experiences of time are distinguished as parts of the consciousness in *Mrs Dalloway* mainly through the authority invested in the notion of clock time, an authority similar to that I ascribed earlier to the causal account of the pin/pain relationship. What Ricoeur demonstrates less well, since he works in search of the aporia, is the co-dependence, if not absolute cooperation between these two facets of time-consciousness. From this point of view, the anachronous arrangement of past events in Clarissa's memory does nothing less than confirm perpetually the chronological order of events from which they digress, and in such a way that the intelligibility of remembered events depends on the reconstruction of their chronological order. The representation of memory, in short, does nothing to question the forward movement of time.

Similar examples of the apparent tension between the 'experience' of time and the true nature of time litter contemporary cultural theory. Once again, it is not a question of belittling the importance of the experience of time in the face of some incontrovertible fact of the cosmos, but rather expanding the notion of experience to encompass the more regulative scientific aspects of time which cultural theorists often banish to some outside space. We might ask, for example, what exactly David Harvey (1989) is asking us to accept about the nature of time when he offers an account of time–space compression. This phenomenon, which in one form or another has been influential on thought about the condition of the contemporary world, is based fundamentally on the increased speed of global communication. Let us look at this argument, which we encountered briefly in Chapter 2, in more detail. While Harvey's account stresses the actual increase in average travel speeds from the age of the horse and the ship to that of jet propelled aviation, others have focused on the virtual and infinite speeds of telecommunications. Harvey's argument describes a process of global contraction in relation to travel speeds, and the significant psychological change that it brings about. If Australia used to be distant in both spatial and temporal terms from Great Britain, the invention of the jet engine has narrowed this temporal distance considerably while leaving spatial distance unchanged. In a similar sense, the spatial distance between Europe and Australia is traversed at infinite speed by the telephone, so that places once months apart are perceived as a simultaneity. These processes are of course enhanced by other developments in technology, and in particular the view of earth from outer space, which encourages a perception of the planet as a whole as a temporal simultaneity. These are very simple arguments, but they have to be taken seriously for their impact on popular experiences of time. It is always possible to follow them into more complex areas. Deleuze, Guattari and Jameson, for example, have linked the condition of time–space compression to the condition of schizophrenia, where the latter is understood in a Lacanian sense, as the collapse of temporal order into simultaneity. For Lacan, schizophrenia is fundamentally a linguistic disorder, in which 'meanings are no longer strung out in time, but are co-present, and in collision with each other. The world, like the sentence, has therefore begun to obey a different temporality in which the controlled admission of differences once ensured by geographical distance is abolished to create a babble of different and co-existing places and cultures. This babble finds its analogy in the co-existence of different moods or mental states experienced in the schizophrenic mind, so that schizophrenia describes a collapse in linear temporality.

Like the threat to the forward motion of time apparently posed by the phenomenon of memory, this set of ideas about time–space compression requires a little more thought. In the first place, it looks as if the phrase itself lacks accuracy, since the compression seems to apply to time and not to space: the number of miles between Britain and Australia is unaltered while the number of minutes is greatly reduced. The phrase is perhaps best understood as amounting to a claim, derived from Einstein's time–space continuum and therefore borrowing from the scientific authority of theoretical physics, that time and space are inseparable. And yet the world is no smaller than it was in 1650, and its contraction must be viewed either in a metaphorical light (the world is like a village), or in relative terms (that it seems small in relation to other scales or to the past). What we have here is another version of the problem of memory's relationship to time, or of the experience of time to actual time. Is the claim that the world is smaller, or is it that the world seems smaller? And to complicate the matter in the way that we did with the last example, we must also ask on what grounds we distinguish between 'is' and 'seems'. This provides a very simple way of describing one of the unreliable tendencies of the so-called 'theory' of postmodernism: that it tends to involve a slippage between the 'seems' and the 'is' without resort to the vast body of theory on this issue that finds its way from Plato through Kant and into phenomenology: the body of theory that we call philosophy.

A good example of an account of the postmodern experience of time, which also takes account of contemporary developments in physics, can be found in the first chapter of Ursula Heise's *Chronoschisms*, 'Narrative and the Postmodern Experience of Time'. This is a survey of ideas about time alongside a set of developments in technology and knowledge that contribute to an altered culture of time, and an account of the postmodern novel as an aesthetic response to that new culture. In addition to Harvey's 'time–space compression' and its dependence on developments in transportation and telecommunications, Heise explores the relevance of television, the computer, the nanosecond as a new unit of time alongside ideas concerned with the end of history, the crisis of historicity that can be found in the new historicisms, the development of subjective time in art and the novel, and the impact of relativity in physics. Some of these subjects receive a more detailed and sustained analytical attention elsewhere, but this is one of the most impressive general surveys of issues relevant to time across the boundaries of science, technology and art. Heise's book also provides a stimulating account of the contemporary novel to complement that offered by Linda Hutcheon, whose notion of 'historiographic metafiction' has acquired so much influence in the theory of the postmodern novel. For my purposes here I want to make a simple observation: that Heise considers a huge range of factors which affect the 'experience of time', and encompasses a range of ideas about time and history, but the philosophy of time is simply missing. It is not that an engagement with the philosophy of time is obligatory for a literary critic, but its absence hinders the discussion and limits the scope of its insights into narrative time. Just as Stephen Hawking desperately needs a first-year university course in metaphysics, if only to be able to state his position on the relationship of the mind to the universe, so too one hears the philosophical coordinates of Heise's discussion calling out to her constantly as she accounts for the relationship between this new culture of time and its encodification in narrative. To put the case simply, it doesn't matter how time behaves in fiction, nor how technology has altered the postmodern experience of time, unless either the representation of time or the experience of time can be related logically, perhaps we should say theoretically, to the nature of time. In the humanities, there is often an untheorised assumption that the nature of time is as described in phenomenology. In Heise's account, the phrase 'postmodern experience of time' operates in two ways. First, it operates phenomenologically in the sense that it locates time not in the universe, but in the universe as it is present to human consciousness; and second, it operates as a kind of collective consciousness, in which the experience of time can be altered by shared conditions such as technological innovation. This is paradigmatic in the humanities, in the sense that there is often an assumption of the constructed nature of the world, of the naivety of the notion of a real world, of reality, or of the fallacy of any position of analytical neutrality which might exist outside the mind, textuality or ideology. From this point of view, the experience of something and the nature of something are inseparable. There is therefore no time other than that experienced in and constructed by the new culture of time, and the efforts of theoretical physics are internal to that culture.

The theoretical basis for this kind of phenomenological presupposition is often farmed out to the theorists of the humanities, such as its philosophers, in much the same way that the philosophical basis of scientific investigation is rarely undertaken by scientists themselves. It has often been noticed that philosophers of science, such as Kuhn (1962) and Popper (2002), advance the most modest accounts of the scientist's access to reality, accounts which do not differ significantly in their presuppositions from the paradigm sketched above: which is to say that they offer a constructivist view of scientific investigation. Kuhn, for example, invests scientific investigation with no greater authority than that of consensus among the those considered to be scientists, a model which was so commensurate with the view of the nature of things in literary theory that it was imported wholesale from the philosophy of science as a theory of methodological revolution for the humanities. In the work of both Kuhn and Popper there is an emphasis on whether scientific analysis works, whether it meets interpretive requirements or whether the knowledge that it yields is falsifiable, but in the work of theoretical physics there is a more strident confidence that the method of investigation is directly related to the physical laws of the universe, which is being discovered and not invented by the analysis. Not even the most preposterous metaphors such as wormholes and black holes will alert the theoretical physicist to the shaping roles of language in general or narrative in particular in relation to these physical laws. The universe has a beginning, a middle and an end, and time is the product of its growth, or expansion, between the big bang and the big crunch.

The question of whether time really exists, and whether it really goes forward, is a little more complicated than the question of whether a physical object exists, but only a little. An approach to this problem will require a brief summary of the question of objects, from transcendental idealism to phenomenology and deconstruction. If we return to the Kantian idea that things in themselves, or noumena, are simply unavailable to human consciousness, and therefore beyond the scope of speculation, we might say the same thing about time: that its actual nature is irrelevant to us, and that we can deal with it only as a phenomenon (in its technical sense, as an experience of an object, or an object for consciousness). The complication is that time is not an object in the same way as a tree, or rather, that it is an object, but it is also a condition from within which we understand objects. For Husserl (1970) and Heidegger

(1962), time and consciousness are categorically inseparable in the sense that we cannot escape the temporal flow of consciousness to reflect upon objects outside of that temporal flow, and least of all on time itself. Kant's bracketing off of the noumenon, or the thing in itself, is a gesture which is repeated throughout modern phenomenology and has come to be known, especially by its critics, as the phenomenological reduction. In Kant's terms, this is the problem of transcendence, and the solution is what he calls, confusingly, the transcendental. If we turn to Husserl, we find him returning to Kant's problem of the transcendent, or the idea of objects as things in themselves which exist outside of the temporal flow of consciousness. Husserl is concerned to show in *Logical Investigations* that the inaccessibility of the outside of consciousness is not catastrophic for the notion of objectivity itself, and that we need only relocate it inside. He does this by developing the concept of intentionality, which he describes as the directedness of consciousness towards an object of which it is conscious, in other words as the internal experience of the outside object. What Kant called the transcendent object, to which we have access only as appearance, is therefore being seen here not as transcendent but as immanent, or inside the consciousness. In the case of a tree, the phenomenological reduction involves the bracketing of the tree, as well as the question of the tree's outside being, to reflect only on the experience of the tree as lived. In the case of time, the phenomenological reduction involves the bracketing of time in itself, as well as the question of the external being and nature of time, to reflect on the experience of time as lived. The immanence of time is a little more complicated than the immanence of a tree because time, understood as the temporal flow of consciousness, is both the subject and the object of reflection, both the consciousness itself and the intention of that consciousness. Husserl tries to get out of this tautological relation of the inside and the outside via the notion of signitive intention. If intention is the directedness of consciousness towards an object, signitive intention is the way that this directedness operates when the object is not present to consciousness; intuition, on the other hand is the kind of intention that is fulfilled by the presence of the object. Here again we have the subject/object distinction located immanently, or within the consciousness, and the distinction allows Husserl to discriminate between a thought about an object, which can take place in the absence of the object, and the direct cognition of the object, or its presence as an intuition in consciousness. What then of the distinction we were working with earlier between phenomenological and cosmological time? It no longer looks adequate to say that a phenomenological approach to time is one which brackets cosmological time to focus on inner consciousness. The phenomenological approach is rather a relocation of cosmological time within the consciousness, as the object intuited by the signitively intended time.

Seen in this light, the tension between the 'seems' and the 'is' which characterises postmodern theory looks rather more interesting. Instead of saying that while the world seems to have shrunk it is in fact the same size, and therefore that appearance has misrepresented reality, we now have to look at the tension not as one between the inner world of mind and the outer world of reality, but as a tension between the sense-making intention of thought (meaning) and the intuition of evidence of the object, both of which are internal to consciousness. In relation to time, then, we have one empty or symbolic notion of time which waits on truth, in the form of evidence of the object, or the intuition of time as an external object or force. Meaning, says Husserl, waits on truth, as intentions of objects wait on the knowledge that fulfils them in the intuition of the presence of the object. The 'seems' of appearance is not indifferent to the evidence or to the objectivity of the object. We might agree with phenomenology that we have access to the reality of time only as an appearance, or an inner lived experience, but in doing so we are not abandoning the ideas of objectivity or evidence. Both the appearance of, and the experience of time are crucially linked to its reality in the same way that the appearance or experience of an object are crucially linked to the transcendent object, but in each case the transcendent object can only be intuited by the 'sense', or made into meaning by the intending consciousness. But the reality of time is a slightly different issue for Husserl as for Kant, from the reality of an object since, in Kant's words 'time is nothing other than the form of inner sense itself' and the 'a priori condition of all appearances'. In other words time is not an object, but it inheres in all objects as they appear to the senses: he therefore maintains the 'empirical reality of time, that is, its objective validity in respect of all objects which allow of ever being given to our senses' while denying to time 'all claim to absolute reality; that is to say, we deny that it belongs to things absolutely, as their condition or property, independent of any reference to the form of our sensible intuition' (Kant 2003: 78). In short, time is all in the mind, as part of the inner form of sense and meaning, but no less real than a tree for it.

Derrida's reading of Husserl is an exciting intervention into this discussion of the inside and the outside of consciousness (Derrida 1973). It does take us away slightly from the question of the reality of time, and yet it also explains how the notion of supplementarity can operate with such apparent disdain for its so-called 'forward' direction. We might begin here with a small sample of Derrida's approach, in general terms, to the relations between inside and outside as spatial metaphors in the discourse of philosophy. One of the recurring schematics in Derridean deconstruction is that of an internal space which is in some way outside its own boundaries. Speaking of Husserl's account of the sign, with its division between indication and expression, Derrida identifies a perplexing logic based on the spatial trope of inside and outside:

> Ex-pression is exteriorization. It imports to a certain outside a sense which is first found on the inside. We suggested above that this outside and this inside were absolutely primordial: the outside is neither nature, nor the world, nor a real exterior relative to consciousness. We can now be more precise. The meaning (bedeuten) intends an outside which is that of an ideal ob-ject. This outside is then ex-pressed and goes forth beyond itself into another outside, which is always 'in' consciousness. (1973: 32)

If sense is Husserl's way of making the distinction between the outside and the inside an immanent one, in the sense of being within consciousness, what Derrida claims here is that the outside, paradoxically and yet also obviously, has been reintroduced on the inside. But this is really only the beginning of the confusion, since the idea of expression is based in an intended outside (or an outside which is within consciousness) which must be sent out beyond itself to another outside, which is still not the outside. Speaking of Plato, Kant, Husserl and Saussure together in *Of Grammatology*, he writes: 'The outside bears with the inside a relationship that is, as usual, anything but simple exteriority. The meaning of the outside was always present within the inside, imprisoned outside the outside and vice versa' (1974: 35). This second example is also part of a discussion of writing conceived as exteriority of consciousness, and this tells us something important about the deconstruction of time. In Derrida's discussions the debate about whether time exists inside of consciousness or outside in the cosmos, or both, or neither, has been recast in such as way that the whole issue of consciousness, with all of its metaphysical baggage, and indeed its very dependence on the idea of interiority (inner consciousness) has been abandoned. In this context, the assertion that *il n'y a pas de hors-texte* must be seen as one that steers us away from consciousness as the realm of immanence in which phenomenological and cosmological time find their existence.

There is something wrong then with a question about the reality of time which is phrased in terms of the inside and the outside of consciousness. This is what Ricoeur has already reminded us, in his caution about the simplistic opposition of internal and clock time. And it may be that it is not simply the category of consciousness that is the problem, but the appeal to spatial objectivity of inside and outside itself. Consider, for example, the relations of inside and outside at work in Derrida's phrase from 'The Law of Genre', 'an internal pocket larger than the whole' (1992: 228). Whereas the general reference of inside and outside depend upon the laws of physics for their meaning, this phrase conveys an impossible object in which the dimensions of an internal space exceed its external dimensions. We might say it serves Kant and Husserl right that the invention of this kind of impossible object can be used as a critique of their adherence to an inside/outside model. It serves them right because the very possibility of creating such an object is the founding gesture of Husserl's account of expression: that the stratum of meaning is analytically separate from the stratum of object intuition. As Derrida loves to point out, in Husserl's analysis it is perfectly possible for a meaning not to wait upon truth, or for its fulfilment in the presence of an external object, and in fact it is the very essence of meaning that it can function in the absence of the object. It is this possibility that leads Derrida to shift from a phenomenology to a grammatology, or an analysis which replaces the whole category of consciousness with that of writing, since writing is meaning which functions in the absence of both the signitive intention (the origin in consciousness) and the intuition of an object (the telos or fulfilment of an intended object). Derrida thus points out that Husserl's system allows perfectly for expression for which no actual or even possible object could be found, such as the expression 'the circle is square'. It is this kind of expression, which makes perfect grammatical sense but for which there can be no outside referent, that deconstructs the teleological account of meaning as object intuition.

The impossible object, and even the impossible world, is of course the very possibility of fiction. Derrida's 'internal pocket larger than the whole' for example, has many fictional equivalents, such as the house in Mark Z. Danielewski's *House of Leaves*, which defies the laws of physics by having internal dimensions which exceed its external dimensions. This is also a useful way of describing the fictional representation of time, since fiction is capable of temporal distortion which cannot be reproduced in lived experience, unless, of course, reading itself can be viewed as lived experience. Though we will, we do not have to turn to fiction to find the impossible. It is central to Derridean deconstruction that this kind of impossibility is a part of the text of philosophy, and the two kinds of impossibility we have been exploring here, of the outside inside and the effect that causes its cause, are actually conditions of its possibility in the same way that we might say that the impossible object or world is the very possibility of fiction. Ricoeur, as we have seen, views the importance of narrative as a kind of discourse in which the intersubjective network of inner time-consciousnesses can be brought into contact with outside forms of time such as cosmological and monumental time, and in which the various aporias that take place between them can find a resolution. My own argument has been that there is a hermeneutic circle between presentification and depresentification that makes us live life as if it weren't present and read fictional narrative as if it were. But here, in Derrida's deconstruction of Husserl, there is a third possibility that might make us look at time in a different way: that fiction, like deconstruction, can present the unpresentable, and can be the impossible, and it is this possibility that gives it a power to subvert Husserl's account that sense waits upon truth in the form of an object present to consciousness.

Derrida's impossible object – the internal pocket which is larger than the whole – offers a model for the relationship between subjective time and objective time in general, as well as a framework for the relationship between the fictional theme of time and the temporal logic of storytelling. If the traditional understanding of subject and object would posit time as divided between the inside and the outside, the time of the mind and the time of the universe, phenomenology, as we have seen, insists that this distinction be relocated on the inside, within consciousness. Time is both the thing that you experience and the way that you experience it. Similarly, in the novel, time is both a matter of content and a matter of form: it is a theme of the novel and it is the logic of storytelling itself. It is to this relationship as it is forged in narrative fiction that the discussion will now turn.

Notes

1. There is a notable exception here in relation to Proust, in which the relations of time and self-consciousness have been the subject of many analyses. But this does not mean that the theoretical or philosophical relations have been established in general, and in a way applicable to other novels. It is at the level of the operations of fiction in general that the neglect is most apparent.
2. This is Nietzsche's example in *The Will to Power*.

Chapter 6

Backwards Time

It is perfectly true, as philosophers say, that life must be understood backwards. But they forget the other proposition that it must be lived forwards.

(Kierkegaard 1999: 3)

In 'The Typology of Detective Fiction', Todorov distinguishes between the whodunit and the thriller on the grounds that the former is a double story and the latter a single one (2000: 139). The whodunit is double in the sense that it is the story of 'the days of the investigation which begin with the crime, and the days of the drama which lead up to it'.[1] The simplicity of this observation is matched only by its importance, because it means that the whodunit goes backwards as it goes forwards, or more precisely that it reconstructs the time line of the crime in the time line of the investigation. In the thriller, on the other hand, the narrative coincides with the action in a single story. The experience of reading the whodunit is characterised by curiosity, since it proceeds from effect to cause, whereas the thriller is characterised by suspense and proceeds from cause to effect.

The hermeneutic circle of presentification and depresentification with which I have been characterising the relationship between reading and living can be seen here at work in the relationship between one type of fiction and another, insofar as the whodunnit works backwards from a known outcome while the thriller proceeds forwards into an unknown future. At first sight, the temporal logic of the whodunit is a paradigm for fiction in general, since the story of the crime unfolds in relation to a future event which is already known and lies in wait, whereas the temporal logic of the thriller is that of life, of an open and unpredictable future. But as is the case for most typological boundaries, this is a difference that is not easy to uphold. In the whodunit, the outcome may be known in the form of the crime, but not in terms of the identity of the culprit, so that we anticipate an unknown future in the whodunit no less than we may, through various forms of analepsis, take excursions into the past in the thriller, making curiosity and suspense a feature of both reading processes. In the case of the whodunit, Todorov also points out that the 'second story'[2] is often told by a narrator who explicitly acknowledges that he is writing a book, or that it is the story of that very book. One of the reasons that the whodunit acts as a kind of typological model for much fiction beyond the genre of the whodunit is that its description seems to work very well for any narrative which involves an interplay between narrated time and the time of the narrative, where the time of the narrative functions as the site of self-conscious reflection both on past events and on the nature of writing about them. This is, after all, the double time of Proust's *In Search of Lost Time*, and one of the recurring features of the *Zeitroman* as it is analysed by Ricoeur (1985).

The idea that moving forwards in time involves a backwards narration is more than just a novelistic structure, and might be thought of, with Proust, as the shape of time itself. It is possible to view ageing itself as a process of acquisition of memories, or the acquisition of a history, after the synchronicity and presence, or the hereness and nowness, of childhood. We have already discussed the phenomenon of archive fever, in which progress into the future is achieved through a continuous archiving of the present in order to relegate events to the past as quickly as possible. The structure of progression as regression, or of forwards and backwards narration, is particularly clear in the case of theoretical physics, in which one of the principal areas of progress over the last century has been the filling out of the story of the history and the origins of the universe, so that progress is made by reconstructing the time line of events leading up to the story which is now being told. We should not be too surprised that theoretical physics, when it translates its sums into narratives, should display the same structural or temporal logic as detective fiction, since the whodunit (perhaps we should say 'whodunit or whatdunit?') is the very structure of narrative explanation in general, whether it operates in fiction or in science. A narrative explanation, as many historiographers have observed, is always an account of the present, and an attempt to dominate the past by understanding it from the point of view of the present, as if progress is a continuous improvement of that understanding.

The detective and the historian share this structure of moving forwards by knowing the past. These two roles are combined with a comic megalomania by Graham Swift's *Waterland*, in which Tom Crick, a fenland history teacher, explains a single incident, the murder of Freddie Parr in the summer of 1943, by reconstructing a time line that goes back to the earliest geological and biological history of the fens and works forwards through the entire family history and the broader social history in which they are embedded: 'It's called reconstructing the crime. From last to first. It's an analogy of the historical method; an analogy of how you discover how you've become what you are' (2002: 312). *Waterland* is a novel which moves forwards by moving backwards, in a process of acquisition of fens history, of Crick history, and of a myriad of stories in general which operate as explanations of events to come. And it is not only the historian's method that produces this temporal loop. History itself proceeds this way:

> It goes in two directions at once. It goes backwards as it goes forwards. It loops. It takes detours. Do not fall into the illusion that history is a well-disciplined and unflagging column marching unswervingly into the future. Do you remember, I asked you – a riddle – how does a man move? One step forward, one step back (and sometimes one step to the side). Is this absurd? No. Because if he never took that step forward –
>
> Or – another of my classroom maxims: There are no compasses for journeying in time. As far as our sense of direction in this unchartable dimension is concerned, we are like lost travellers in a desert. We believe we are going forward, towards the oasis of Utopia. But how do we know – only some imaginary figure looking down from the sky (let's call him God) can know – that we are not moving in a great circle. (1984: 135)

This narrator knows what he thinks about time, and regularly formulates theses such as this which underlie the narrative form of the story itself. *Waterland* is therefore a novel full of explicit theorisation which finds its application in the storytelling itself: a novel which explores the theme of time through the temporal logic of storytelling. To this effect, the possibility that we are moving backwards, or in a great circle, when we think we are progressing forwards is pitched against the view of time as a river, or as the flow of water, with which it has been associated since well before Plato. The explicit theorising, or philosophising, about time in *Waterland* is typical of a certain kind of contemporary novel, and the discussion that follows aims to identify, diagnose and explain what it is that the contemporary novel has to tell us, if anything, about time.

However much the novel might philosophise explicitly on the subject of time, its difference from philosophy is marked by narrative form. The novelistic treatment of the question of time differs from the philosophical treatment in having at its disposal all the temporal resources of narrative fiction as a complement to the resources of reasoned argument. If a philosophical discourse is fundamentally constative in its approach to time, in the sense that it makes arguments and statements which may be judged true or false on the subject of time, the narrative fiction is fundamentally capable of being constative and performative at the same time. Of course a novel might not openly philosophise about time, and equally might not deploy its temporal resources in any notable way: such a novel might be thought, at the constative and the performative level, to be a novel which is not about time.[3] But the focus of the first part of this discussion will be on the contemporary novel which explores the theme of time in both constative and performative ways. In this light we might ask whether the explicit philosophising about time in *Waterland* is in some way corroborated by the temporal structure of its narrative. The example above poses the question of the direction of time in terms of a tension between circular and linear understandings of time, as well as the apparent contradiciton between forwards and backwards motion. If this is the explicit reflection from the narrator, it takes little effort to establish that this is also the temporal structure of the narrative, and therefore that the narrator's reflective commentary and his method of storytelling exist in a relation of mutual corroboration. If the entire span of narrated events is taken into account, the chronological sequence of *Waterland* begins in prehistory and ends in 1979, yet the novel begins and ends in 1943. The events of 1943 are explained by a considerable quantity of historical detail, particularly Crick family history from the mid-eighteenth century, and in turn offer an explanation of events subsequent to 1943, and ultimately for Tom's predicament in the time locus of the narrator in 1979. This impressive chain of explanation is constructed through a kind of perpetual anachrony as the narrator refers forwards and backwards from the novel's central events. The corroboration in question, between the philosophy of time that the novel advances through the mouthpiece of its historian narrator and the method of storytelling employed by that narrator is explicated in passages of commentary which repeatedly link the question of history with the mode of narrative both in general, and in relation to this specific narrative itself. The philosophy of time which views history as backwards and forwards motion is both enacted by and explicitly linked to the anachronistic temporal structure of the narrative. In fact the constative and the performative modes of *Waterland*'s consideration of time – this cooperation between narrative commentary and fictional form – should be understood as nothing more than self-analysis: as the narrator contemplates the structure of his own story he is at the same time directed into flights of speculation about the connection of self-narration to history, about the cyclical nature of history in general, and about the shape of time.

If the theme of time and the temporal logic of storytelling seem to be inseparable here, we ought not to view this as a necessary condition. It is only necessary to think of Sterne's *Tristram Shandy*, or of Rushdie's

Midnight's Children, to recognise that a novel is equally capable of espousing one view of time while performing another. But for *Waterland*, the corroboration is apparently absolute, and particularly so because the reciprocity between the novel's formal structure and its explicit theorisation of time is largely forged by its tropological system, according to which the landscape of the fens, and in particular its rivers, provides a symbolic landscape through which philosophical arguments about time and narrative can be advanced. Hence, the discovery of Freddie's body in the lock in July 1943 – that singular event around which the novel's whole chain of narrative explanation is constructed – offers the lock as the analogue for a moment of presence, in which the flow of the river is artificially arrested. The novel's images of water, particularly those of the irreversible flow of water, of rivers that cannot flow upwards, and of water being pumped upwards for the purposes of land reclamation assemble an allegorical network for the representation of, among other things, incest, explanation and the relationship between fact and fiction. Cleverly, even the circularity of time can be incoporated by the metaphor of the river:

> The Ouse flows on, unconcerned with ambition, whether local or national. It flows now in more than one channel, its waters diverging, its strength divided, silt-prone, flood-prone. Yet it flows – oozes – on, as every river must, to the sea. And, as we all know, the sun and the wind suck up the water from the sea and disperse it on the land, perpetually refeeding the rivers. So that while the Ouse flows to the sea, it flows, in reality, like all rivers, only back to itself, to its own source; and that impression that a river moves only one way is an illusion. And it is only an illusion that what you throw (or push) into a river will be carried away, swallowed for ever, and never return. And that remark first put about, two and a half thousand years ago, by Heraclitus of Ephesus, that we cannot step twice into the same river, is not to be trusted. Because we are always stepping into the same river. (145–6)

Such metaphors for the movement of time, in this case operating against the ordinary conception on time, require no great interpretative effort on the part of the reader. The narrator's own commentary performs much of the interpretative work to identify the philosophical, or doctrinal, function of images drawn from the East Anglian landscape. As a result of this self-conscious, self-interpreting commentary, the novel's rivers belong no more to the literal content of the work than they do to the explicit theorisation of time, and the relation of reciprocity which exists between *Waterland*'s narrative form and its theory of time, these images acquire a double function, representing both the operations of the narrative itself, and the philosophy of time it advances. From this point of view, what the novel says about time and what it does with the arrangement of its plot, with its loops and detours, are forged together like the vehicle and tenor or an elaborate metaphorical landscape.

Rejecting Chronology

What we have in *Waterland* then is an explicit discourse on the subject of time, working alongside a narrative form which corroborates and reflects its observations. This cooperation of the constative and performative is strengthened at the level of imagery which carries a set of doctrines about time and which is also the subject of an explicit interpretative commentary which decodes the novel's metaphors into theoretical propositions about time. The novel presents something more associative, more layered and less logocentric than the straightforward constative statements that characterise analytical and philosophical approaches to time. It may be that the presentation is of something more logically vague: *Waterland* may not be sure exactly what it thinks about time, and it may be saying several different things about time at the same time. In the two citations above, for example, a central plank of the claim about time, articulated in the first place in explicit commentary and in the second instance by the metaphor of the circular river, is that it might be an illusion to view time in linear and monodirectional ways. We are, in the terms of the first example, like travellers lost in the desert, who think they are moving forwards when in fact they are moving in an enormous circle, and in terms of the second, we are misled by the appearance that a river moves in one direction to the sea, since, viewed from a greater distance, the line is a circle. Interesting though this proposition is, it ought not to be viewed as a startling one in the context of a novel. It could be more persuasively argued, perhaps, that this is the most standard, most conventional proposition that a novel advances about time: that the linearity of clock time is somehow placed in question by the circularity of some version of mind time, whether it be recollection, the explanation of a detective or the anachronicity of plot more generally. The novel, characteristically and typically, produces a tension between the chronology of events it describes and the anachronicity of their representation in the mind of a character, or of the plot itself. This is exactly where the power of the novel lies, according to Ricoeur and others. The philosophy of time, for Ricoeur, will always run up against some version of the dichotomy between clock time and mind time and experience this dichotomy as a kind of aporia. The philosophy of time from Zeno to Derrida can be read as a failure to escape the tensions involved in these aporias, or to banish the dualism from which they derive. But these tensions and aporias are the very fabric of the novel: the tensions between narrated time and the time of the narration, chronology and plot, objective and subjective time, cosmological and phenomenological time, time as topic and time as technique, and the constative and performative layering of the novel's dealings with time make it the discourse in which the dynamics and dialectics of time are most faithfully and properly observed.

It might seem reasonable to suppose that contemporary fiction has something new to say about time insofar as these temporal tensions have been placed in the foreground and openly contemplated. But Ricoeur has a warning here which is, I think, much more complicated than it sounds:

> Rejecting chronology is one thing, the refusal of any substitute principle of configuration is another. It is not conceivable that the narrative should have moved beyond all configuration. The time of the novel may break away from real time. In fact, this is the law for the beginning of any fiction. But it cannot help but be configured in terms of new norms of temporal organization that are still perceived as temporal by the reader, by means of new expectations regarding the time of fiction . . . To believe that we are done with the time of fiction because we have overturned, disarticulated, reversed, telescoped, or reduplicated the temporal modalities the conventional paradigms of the novel have made familiar to us, is to believe that the only time conceivable is precisely chronological time. It is to doubt that fiction has its own resources for inventing temporal measurements proper to it. It is also to doubt that these resources encounter expectations in the reader concerning time that are infinitely more subtle than rectilinear succession. (1985: 25)

The simple point here is that novels which are experimental in their use of time are, at best, establishing new novelistic conventions for the configuration of time, and at worst, actually reaffirming the notion of real time as rectilinear succession. It would be foolish to assume that the detours and loops involved in the narration of *Waterland* present any real challenge to the predominance of chronology as a model of time. In fact it would be safer to claim that the active efforts of a reader in the reconstruction of a time line function to reinforce linear causality in a novel like *Waterland*, the active reconstruction of causation and succession being more participatory than the passive mode in which the reader receives a linear plot. (The claim that *Waterland* is establishing 'new norms of temporal organization' would be an inflated one, and somewhat out of line with the novel's own tenets about time and its self-knowledge as a conventional story.) The complication of this warning, however, lies in the notion of 'configuration' itself. A novel, says Ricoeur, 'may break away from real time', but it cannot break away from configuration. This is an important argument for my discussion here because it helps to define the way in which a novel might both say and do something new in relation to time.

Ricoeur's account of configuration is introduced in Volume 1 of *Time and Narrative* and plays a prominent part in his account of mimesis. Configuration is the central and most important part (mimesis 2) of the three stages of mimesis proposed by Ricoeur and is derived from Aristotle's notion of muthos or 'emplotment': it is, in Aristotle's words, the 'organization of events'. The interesting thing about configuration in relation to time is that it takes its place in a hermeneutic circle whereby the organisation of events in a narrative fiction modifies the understanding that a reader may have of real time, and this changed understanding in effect comes to be part of the world of action which subsequent narrative fictions may then reflect. This circle of prefiguration, configuration and refiguration might also be understood as a concept of mimesis coupled to a concept of reverse mimesis, according to which a fiction may be seen to imitate the world of action and in so doing, produces a reverse mimesis in which the world of action 'imitates', or is modified by, fiction. In terms of time, this means that the temporality of fiction both reflects and produces the temporality of, for want of a better word, 'life': a kind of spiralling movement in which the fictional representation of time and the lived experience of time constantly modify each other. If this is so, how are we to make sense of the argument, offered in the previous paragraph, that a novel may break away from real time, but that it cannot break away from configuration? This would be to say that the emplotment of a novel – let us say the fragmented analeptic and proleptic excesses of *Waterland*'s organisation of events – may depart from the 'real time' of chronological succession, but it cannot break away from temporal organisation in itself. The problem with this is that it seems to be ontologically undecided on the question of whether real time belongs within configuration or lies outside it. On one hand, there seems to be an absolute presupposition that real time is chronological, and that this chronology underlies the conventional paradigms of the novel. On the other hand, the hermeneutic circle insists that the temporality of life is in turn an imitation of the temporality of fiction, and therefore that chronology is nothing other than configuration refigured. Ricoeur seems to be, on the one hand the phenomenologist who views time experience as the horizon of its reality and on the other hand to be offering the notion of real time as the referent which lies beyond that horizon. If Derrida's critique of Husserl is that his theory of meaning constantly reintroduces the opposition of inside and outside of consciousness which the phenomenological reduction seeks to displace, my objection to Ricoeur is that for all the flag waving, his declared allegiance to the phenomenology of time-consciousness, his argument repeatedly reintroduces the idea of chronology as the outside of temporality.

This is important for the relationship between what a novel says about time and what it does. For Ricoeur, the very idea of a novel *about* time is bound up with the question of reference. Following Benveniste, he takes the view that the critique of reference, which is found in and follows from the work of Saussure, does not apply to the larger units of discourse from the sentence upwards: 'With the sentence, language is oriented beyond itself. It says something *about* something' (1984–8: 78; his italics). This is not a position on reference that I would reject, but the claim that language from the sentence upwards says something *about* something becomes confusing when that something is time. In Chapter 5 I considered the question of the inside and the outside of consciousness, and in particular the paradoxical relation between the mind and the universe that is posited in phenomenology: that time is a river which sweeps me along, but I am the river, as Borges puts it (1964: 187). In less metaphorical language, this posits an account of time as an external, mind-independent medium which we live within at the same time as it posits the absolute internality of time to consciousness. The thing I am inside is inside me, just as the universe is something I am within and yet its only being is within my consciousness. If, with Heidegger, we were to view temporality not simply as internal time-consciousness but, in Derrida's phrase, the 'internal pocket which is larger than the whole', that is the thing which is inside us but of which we are a part, there can be no time which exists on the outside of temporality, since temporality in a sense names exactly the aporia of the inside and the outside. But for Ricoeur, the dialectic of time and narrative, the hermeneutic circle of their relationship, cannot operate from the Heideggerean position, and a certain distance from this position is required for the whole idea of a narrative which is *about* time to operate. For Ricoeur, the human sciences, and he names history and narratology (1984–8: 86), and indeed the physical sciences, would be disabled by the Borgesian or the Heideggerean aporia. Temporality, in Ricoeur's study requires an outside – a real time – to which language in its discursive units above the level of the sentence refers. This is the way that the term 'chronology' operates throughout the argument, as the outside of temporality:

> If it is true that the major tendency of modern theory of narrative – in historiography and the philosophy of history as well as in narratology – is to 'dechronologize' narrative, the struggle against the linear representation of time does not necessarily have as its sole outcome the turning of narrative into 'logic', but rather may deepen its temporality. Chronology – or

chronography – does not have just one contrary, the a-chronology of laws or models. Its true contrary is temporality itself. (1984–8: 30)

If temporality is, as it must be, human time-consciousness, chronology, as its contrary, appears to take on the role of something more objective or cosmological here: something that exists on the outside of language, of discourse and of the mind. But if this is true, if chronology is the outside of human temporality, it takes on a rather contradictory set of meanings in relation to the novel, and specifically in relation to Aristotelian emplotment or Ricoeur's configuration: chronology is real time and it is realistic configuration of discourse; it is the truth of the cosmos and the configuration which faithfully represents that truth. It is this unacknowledged doubleness of chronology, as both inside and outside the temporality of configuration, that makes Ricoeur's earlier statement – that the novel can break away from real time, but cannot break away from configuration – rather ambiguous (1984). The rejection of chronology in the contemporary novel, according to this ambiguity, becomes more than the mere rejection of an established set of norms that govern temporal organisation, since those norms are faithful to the laws that govern the universe. The notion of fiction which is *about* something, and specifically fiction which is *about time*, seems to demand this oscillation between the hermeneutic phenomenology which views chronology itself as a kind of emplotment, and the realism which views it as a brute fact of the universe. This oscillation can be seen as a model for a more general polarity in critical responses to novels about time, at one pole of which is the view that the novel has the power to ridicule the efforts of the physical sciences to comprehend time, and at the other, a belief in the absolute authority of the physical sciences in relation to which the novel attempts its imaginative alternatives.

In what relation do these imaginative alternatives stand to the chronological configurations of the conventional novel, and indeed to the chronological configurations of the cosmos? The novel which depends heavily on analeptic and proleptic anachronies appears, above all, to confirm the intimate relation between chronology and sense, since the reader's act of sense-making involves the rearrangement of events into a linear succession. In the case of *Waterland*, there is the intricate reconstruction of the time line in which events in 1947, encountered on a first reading in fragments, become intelligible. In the case of Martin Amis's *Time's Arrow*, the effort to make sense of events narrated backwards often involves a strikingly literal kind of inversion of the inversion, such as the reading of letters from right to left, or of dialogue upwards on the page, in order to reconstruct the causal chain which is the basis of its intelligibility. Are we then to assume that the primary function of the fictional rejection of chronology is the affirmation of chronology. Given that the forward linearity of time ranks among the very highest of absolute human presuppositions, can we really attribute one of the principal characteristics of contemporary fiction to such a statement of the obvious, or such an affirmation of the presupposed? The stronger claim, which I have been rehearsing over the last few paragraphs, is that the novel is ultimately faithful to temporality rather than chronology, or that it rejects chronology in order to affirm a phenomenology of time-consciousness. According to this claim, the analepses and prolepses of contemporary fiction might reflect a valorisation of mind time, an experience of time which subordinates the cosmological to the phenomenological, and which views chronology as a kind of noumenology without foundation. But this is not a satisfactory account either. It is just possible that the rejection of chronology in the Modernist novel might be viewed in this way as a rejection of external in favour of internal reality, and therefore as a shift from cosmological to phenomenological time. But as I argued in Chapter 5 in relation to *Mrs Dalloway*, the temporality of indirect discourse, stream of consciousness or interior monologue, for all its temporal jumping, does not conform to Genette's account of narrative anachrony. The recollections and anticipations of Clarissa Dalloway or Molly Bloom are not proleptic and analeptic as such, since the discourse faithfully adheres to a linear sequence of thoughts, and makes no excursions into the past or future out of turn. The contemporary novel, on the other hand, though it has preserved this interest in subjective reality and continued to develop means of rendering it, has been preoccupied with narrative anachrony of a more traditional kind, in the sense that it develops a preoccupation with such excursions into the past or future of a sequence, and likes to flaunt the freedom of the novel to roam in time. The explanation for this preoccupation does not lie in the rejection of chronology at some level of philosophical conviction, but in the relationship between narrative and explanation. Life, as Kierkegaard says, must be understood backwards but lived forwards. If philosophers tend to forget the second half of this adage, the proleptic novel effectively joins the forward motion of lived experience with the backward movement of narrative explanation.

From this point of view the rejection of chronology is not really about time in the sense that it places in question the forward motion of time as rectilinear succession. Rather it arranges events in such a way that the gap between the forward motion of life and the backwards motion of explanation are articulated to each other. Once again, it is the

incorporation of self-distance within the lived present, and most significantly the installation of future retrospect in present experience, in which
we find the most convincing explanation of the new norms of temporal
organisation in the novel.

In *Waterland*, what the novel says about time is infinitely less interesting than what it does in the service of depresentifying, or installing future
retrospect in the account it gives of the present. The following passage
represents a typical strategy:

> Why did fear transfix me at that moment when the boathook clawed at
> Freddie Parr's half-suspended body? Because I saw death? Or the image of
> something worse? Because this wasn't just plain, ordinary, terrible, unlooked-
> for death, but something more?
>   Children, evil isn't something that happens far off – it suddenly touches
> your arm. I was scared when I saw the dark blood appear but not flow in the
> gash on Freddie's head. But not half so scared as when Mary Metcalf said to
> me later that day: 'I told him it was Freddie. Dick killed Freddie Parr because
> he thought it was him. Which means we're to blame too.' (2002: 35)

The dialogue that closes this passage is extracted from a scene which is
still to be narrated in full (2002: 57) in which it becomes clear that Dick
killed Freddie because Mary led Dick to believe that Freddie was the
father of her unborn child. This is in effect an excursion forward to the
answer to the mystery which faces the reader in this scene, but it is a
cryptic visitation from the future, in which the referent of 'it' in 'I told
him it was Freddie' is as yet unknown. It is a glimpse of the future which
identifies the killer but not the motive. The narration of one moment,
the discovery of Freddie's body, has installed in it a moment which is,
in chronological terms, to occur later that day, and for which the reader
will have to wait twenty-two pages. This is one of the teleological projections which is built into the narrative voice, which was referred to in
Chapter 3 as Prolepsis 1. A second kind of juxtaposition of moments
occurs between the moment being narrated in 1943 and the time of its
narration in 1979, that is the moment of Tom Crick's final class to his
children, of which *Waterland* is the text. This is Prolepsis 2, that is the
foregrounding of the structural retrospect of the novel as a whole
through reference to the here and now of the time locus of narration,
achieved in this passage by the direct address to his audience as
'Children' at the start of the second paragraph. Though it is absent in
this passage, the novel is also pervaded with instances of Prolepsis 3,
most obviously whenever Tom deals with an objection from Price, the
novel's surrogate reader, who regularly articulates within the story
objections to Tom's mode of historical explanation, which represent

possible objections on the part of an external reader, and which can therefore be precluded. In this way, the present of past events, which a less proleptic narrative would presence, or presentify, according to the conventions of linear retrospect, is never permitted, in *Waterland* to escape from the teleological retrospect which these various forms of prolepsis build into narrated events. Every moment is looked back upon whether from the moment of its narration or from any other point between the time locus of the narration and the time locus of the narrated. If reading novels encourages us to experience the present as the object of a future memory, this relationship can also be internalised in the novel by prolepsis, which articulates any past moment to some known moment subsequent to it, in a constant repetition of the hermeneutic circle of presentification and depresentification. As if the structure of detective fiction were not in itself enough, or that it demanded too much patience on the part of the reader, prolepsis joins the backwards movement of explanation to the forwards movement of life in a way that seems to deprive us of the unmediated presence of fictional events, installing in the present a position of future retrospect from which an explanation of the present might be possible.

If *Waterland* repeatedly offers us a present structured as the anticipation of retrospect, it also offers its converse, in the form of remembered anticipation. At the novel's climactic moment, in which Dick plunges to his death, the event's presence is compromised in the narrator's memory: 'Memory can't even be sure whether what I saw, I saw first in anticipation before I actually saw it, as if I had witnessed it somewhere already – a memory before it occurred' (2002: 356). The narrator is actually describing here, in the experience of a moment, what the narrative constantly performs: the installation of a future memory within the moment. In this case, there is some uncertainty, since the memory of the event cannot distinguish for certain between the anticipation of retrospect and the actual retrospect to which the event is immediately consigned. If *Waterland* consistently performs what it attempts to say about time, it also seems to try to blur the distinction between saying and doing, or between the constative and performative proposition about time, and in this case, that blurring is achieved by the impossibility of separating the anticipation of a memory from the memory of an anticipation. It is clear that this blurring of actual and envisaged retrospect deprives this climactic moment of its presence, sandwiching the moment, as it does, between the forward movement of an anticipation and the backward movement of a recollection, so that once again the co-dependence of time and self-distance comes into view.

Time's Arrow and Self-Distance

The relationship between self-distance and time, which is forged in prolepsis, is starkly demonstrated by fiction in which time runs backwards. Saint Augustine's *Confessions*, I have argued, offers an allegory about the temporality of first-person narration which runs alongside, and perhaps produces his explicit reflections on time, but all self-narration is about time and self-distance, since the word *about* is in itself incapable of the theoretical work which might separate the logic from the theme of storytelling. There is always an element of self-distance in first-person narration in the sense that it creates a schism between the narrator and the narrated, though they are the same person, and in this schism, there is often a cooperation between temporal and moral self-distance which allows for the self-judgement of retrospect. In Amis's *Time's Arrow*, the disjunction between the narrator and the narrated, however, is not a difference of location in time, but one of the experience of the direction of time. This is self-distance taken to an extreme, and often seems to function as a parody of the more conventional temporal logic of confession. In confession there is a moral contrast between the narrator and the narrated, but when the narrator is travelling backwards through the same life that the narrated lived forwards, the moral distance could not be greater. In moral terms, this is true opposition, understood as the maximum of difference, since when cause and effect are reversed, everything that is good becomes bad and vice versa.

There is a strong case that this is not properly thought of as self-narration at all. The narrator in *Time's Arrow* is a kind of doppelganger: a fellow traveller in Tod Friendly's body barely connected to, and incapable of understanding, the character who lived the narrated events in the opposite direction. This means that while conventional self-narration offers a special kind of inside view, based in recollection, self-witnessing, and self-representation, this self-narrator has no access to the thought processes of the narrated character. Just as the schism of moral self-distance in conventional self-narration is ironically exaggerated by this device, so too, the theme of unreliability which so often dominates the traditional first-person story is here given an extreme expression in the form of a narrative in which the narrator and the narrated, though sharing a body, are complete strangers: the authoritative yet unreliable inside view has been ironically exaggerated into a world of self-knowledge dominated by misunderstanding and the impossibility of the inside view. The conventional pronouns of first-person narration also become ironically transposed, as the schism of self-reference in the third person is literalised into the self-reference between two secret sharers.

In the first few pages of the narrative the pronouns shift from first-person singular to first-person plural, and then to the consistent self-reference in the third person which operates throughout much of the novel. Tod becomes the name of the narrated, but not of the narrator. Whereas in the confessional narrative, the narrator and the narrated cannot coincide in time, since there will then be nothing to narrate except narration itself, for the I and the Tod of this narrative, there is a period of co-incidence (Chapters 5 and 6) as forwards and backwards time meet halfway, in Auschwitz, when the unity of the I is restored, and in which everything starts to make sense. Again, the opposition of forwards and backwards time produces a species of parodic irony in which the pronoun usage of conventional self-narration is defamiliarised.

It is well known, because it is written in the novel's 'Afterword', that one source of inspiration for Amis's narrative technique came from the famous backwards paragraph of Kurt Vonnegut's *Slaughterhouse Five*, in which a backwards-running Second World War film transforms the destruction of a bombing raid into an act of humanitarian repair. In this paragraph, and in the early parts of Amis's novel, the reversal of time produces both comic and serious effects. If the reversal of cause and effect produces a moral inversion in which everything good becomes bad and vice versa, the humour of inversion itself becomes a form of moral critique. Amis's novel turns many of our domestic habits and social institutions into absurdities and atrocities, especially in those cases where the forward motion of repair is inverted into an act of destruction. The most obvious example here is in the atrocity performed by hospitals in the postwar period of Tod's life, and the moral contrast that these atrocities present to the narrator when compared to the miracles of Aushwitz, and its project to 'make a people from the weather' (128). Running backwards, the postwar hospital is an awful institution with no end of cruelties to perpetrate:

> Some guy comes in with a bandage around his head. We don't mess about. We'll soon have that off. He's got a hole in his head. So what do we do. We stick a nail in it. Get a nail – a good rusty one – from the trash or wherever. And lead him out to the Waiting Room where he's allowed to linger and holler for a while before we ferry him back to the night. (85)

This is the novel's one joke, which it tells repeatedly in a number of forms, as it leads up to the central atrocity of Auschwitz. The fact that it is a joke leading towards Auschwitz is enough to indicate the serious moral purpose of its humour. This is a narrator rendered so unreliable by his inverted experience of time that he misreads Auschwitz as a miracle and postwar medicine as an atrocity. The moral distance between the narrator and the narrated, which characterises the confessional narrative is here transformed into an extreme of ironic moral distance, according to which the reader must translate the narrator's every moral judgement into its opposite. This readerly participation in the reconstruction of the real time line also involves the reader in a perception, or a realisation, that the directionality of time is implicit in other aspects of our conceptual structure, and that the notion of moral action is rendered meaningless when the forward motion of time is inverted. Even in the case of the most morally neutral actions the novel shows that our conceptual structure is somehow dependent on the direction of time: a tennis rally which ends with the arbitrary pocketing of a ball is deprived of its competitive drive; a traffic system in which everybody drives backwards empties the act of driving of all free will. It is, in other words, far more than morality which is at stake in the inversion of time. Since the 1960s, physicists have theorised about the possibility of backwards time which seems inherent in the notion of an expanding universe, but often have to retreat from the conceptualisation of a world running backwards on the basis of its absolute unintelligibility to the mind which is adapted to the forward motion of time:

> The arrow of time is so powerful and pervasive that its reversal would leave any being stuck with forward-time perception nonplussed and helpless. Imagine witnessing broken eggs reassembling themselves as if by a miracle, water running uphill, snow melting into snowmen, water in unheated pans spontaneously boiling, and so on. These processes would not merely seem unnerving and surprising, they would strike at the very heart of rationality. Prediction and memory play a vital part in all our activities, and a being who found these faculties operating the wrong way relative to the outside world would be utterly helpless. (Davis 1995: 222)

The injunction to imagine such a world is the starting point of Amis's novel, and the effect is not only to show the utter helplessness of such a person, but to place every reader in such a position of utter helplessness from which the defence of rationality must entail the reassertion of forwards time. It is, in other words, not only the physicist who retreats from the unintelligibility of a backwards world. But whereas the physicist tends to view the second law of thermodynamics as a foundation for the forward motion of time, others prefer to view the laws of thermodynamics, according to which the entropy of a closed system of energy can only increase and never decrease, as merely an instance of time's asymmetry in our system of rationality. Hence, in Richard Menke's reading of the novel (1998), the notion of time's arrow, as it is understood in A. S. Eddington's *The Nature of the Physical World*, is a field of metaphor which the novel uses to demonstrate the dependence of other aspects of rationality, such as historical understanding, on forward-time perception, rather than as its determining law. Similarly, in the philosophy of time, the laws of thermodynamics are generally understood as a co-dependent aspect of a conceptual system, without according foundational importance to them.[4] Paul Horwich, for example, in *Asymmetries in Time*, includes the laws of thermodynamics in a list of ten temporally asymmetric phenomena which operate in our conceptual system.[5] Seen in this way, where the irreversibility of time is inseparable from rationality itself, the argument against backwards time tends to be expressed in terms of consequences, or the fear that time reversal is paramount to irrationality. J. R. Lucas, for example, argues that the conceptual cost of time reversal is very high indeed:

> A world in which we could, like the White Queen, remember the future and could alter the past would be one in which our ordinary concepts of memory, knowledge, explanation, aspiration, ambition, action and achievement would be inapplicable. Although attempts have been made to account for these conceptual asymmetries, as well as our experience of the passing of time, by reference to the Second Law of Thermodynamics, which in turn is alleged to stem from the initial conditions which happened to obtain at the time of the Big Bang, the enterprise is uncalled for and unsuccessful. Scientists have abstracted from our ordinary conception of time a surrogate that is not only homogeneous but isotropic, and have then sought to put back into the new concept the directedness that they had removed from the old. But the Second Law of Thermodynamics, though of great significance for our understanding of time, cannot explain all time-directed phenomena . . . nor can itself be derived from purely fortuitous factors obtaining at the dawn of creation. (1989: 5–6)

Time reversal may begin as a joke, and may read like a joke, but as the novel sets out to demonstrate in its movement from comic set-pieces to the undoing of Auschwitz, not only because morality is inverted. The conceptual cost of backwards time is so high that it must be contained in fiction, in order to specify the distance between fiction and the rational world. In the arguments of Menke, Horwich and Lucas there is also a subversion of the foundational importance of the second law of thermodynamics which suggests that we might as well consider narrative order to be determined by the second law of thermodynamics as consider the second law of thermodynamics to be the mere elaboration of narrative order, and view it, along with the Big Bang, as nothing more than a story.

Time's Arrow demonstrates the conceptual consequences of time reversal at a level of detail for which the philosopher has no patience. But the key word here is 'demonstrate'. *Time's Arrow* is more performative than constative in its inquiry into time, tirelessly demonstrating the absurdity of a backwards universe without staking any claims about time, and so without risking the adjudication of its knowledge on the basis of truth. It is therefore impossible to know, and pointless to ask, which aspects of this demonstration are conscious and which are accidental consequences of time reversal. The effect of time reversal that *Time's Arrow* seems least in control of is the relationship between the meaning of words and the forward direction of time. There is a sense in which the novel has compromised on time reversal from the start, demonstrating at first a rigorous inversion of the phonetic structure of words ('Oo y'rrah?' = 'How are you?') before retreating to a more readable blend between forward and backward movement. It is clear that the direction of reading, from left to right within a word or sentence, from the top to the bottom of a page, and from the left to the right page, must be preserved in order for linguistic significance to survive at all. Even at a less literal level, the reversal of time deprives words of their sense, whenever those words refer to a temporal process:

> Around midnight sometimes, Tod Friendly will create things. Wildly he will mend and heal. Taking hold of the woodwork and the webbing, with a single blow to the floor, with a single impact, he will create a kitchen chair. With one fierce and skilful kick of his aching foot he will mend a deep concavity in the refrigerator's flank. With a butt of his head he will heal the fissured bathroom mirror, heal also the worsening welt in his own tarnished brow, and then stand there staring at himself with his eyes flickering. (63)

The words 'create', 'mend' and 'heal' refer to acts conventionally designated with words such as 'destroy', 'damage' and 'wound', but there is no logical reason that this should be so. The narrator and Tod are, in the mind of the narrator, living life in the same direction, since the narrator's backwards time is produced by the perception that time for everything and everyone else is also reversed. The arbitrary relation between a signifier and a signified functions just we well in backwards time as it does in forwards time, so that the word 'mend' can be used to designate either the act of damaging or repairing a refrigerator. According to this argument, 'mend' will mean something positive to Tod and negative to the narrator: the signifier will be shared but the signifieds will diverge into opposition according to the difference between the conceptual structures of forwards and backwards time. The novel does not, and in fact could not use language in this way, and requires us instead to ignore the fact that between the narrator's language and Tod's, there is no possibility of comprehension.

The narrator, in other words, is stuck with a language in which the meaning of words in general, and the positive valences of words such as 'mend', are adapted to the forward motion of time, so that the very words he uses to describe the backward movement of time have inscribed in them the impossibility of that movement. Even more than for the backward phonetic structure of 'Oo y'rrah', which can simply be read backwards, what is in question here is the intelligibility of language itself. The use of a forward-moving language for the description of backwards time is in fact necessary for the perception of any moral difference between Tod and the narrator, since the rigorous representation of backwardness, in which the same signifier was used to represent divergent, or even opposite, signifieds would render the difference between forwards and backwards time as invisible as the signified is invisible behind the signifier in general. The semantic compromise, like the phonetic one, might be viewed as necessary for the readability of the text, but this is not some innocent or pragmatic decision. It is paramount to the recognition that the forward motion of time is embedded in language itself, and not merely one aspect of conceptual structure which can happily co-exist with others. In fact, *Time's Arrow* seems above all to generate confusion out of the tension between the forward motion of language and the supposed backwardness of time that it represents. Why, for example, should the narrator think that Mikio, who is Japanese, reads a book in the same way as he does, and that they are in the minority in doing so? If the narrator is living backwards, and therefore perceiving the world in backwards time, it is the majority of Americans and Europeans who will read in the same direction as the narrator, and Mikio's reading would still appear different. To assume otherwise is to assume that the narrator himself perceives his difference from forward-living people, and therefore destroys the narrative's most basic assumption that he is unwittingly experiencing time in reverse. How can this narrator say of Mikio's reading practice that he 'begins at the beginning and ends at the end' (51) if the implication is that others begin at the end and end at the beginning, an implication which would also destroy the narrative's most basic assumption. This is not a problem that Vonnegut faced in his famous backwards paragraph in *Slaughterhouse Five*, because there is no inconsistency between language and temporal reference when a forward-orientated language system describes a backward-running film. The problem only arises when the temporality of consciousness itself is imagined in reverse, because the language which purports to describe it is itself the direction of time for consciousness. From this point of view, *Time's Arrow* offers a striking example of a contradiction between what the novel does and what it says. In the attempt to represent backwards time, the novel constantly affirms the forward direction of time and this is not only because the reader must participate in the reconstruction of events in the opposite direction in order to understand them. There is something more fundamentally wrong with a backwards narration which suggests that the forward motion of time and the forward motion of language together might be the very basis of intelligibility of our words and concepts.

Notes

1. These words belong to George Burton's novel *Passing Time* in which an authorial voice explains the nature of detective fiction to his narrator.
2. Todorov calls the story of events which begin with the crime, or the story of the investigation, the 'second story' because it is chronologically posterior to the story of events which lead up to the crime, but in the terminology I was borrowing from Genette in Chapter 3, the investigation would be the first story in relation to which the events which lead up to the crime would be analeptic.
3. I refer the reader here to the discussion of 'aboutness' in Chapter 1 of this volume, which outlines the danger of thinking that the conventional novel is not about time simply because it produces a more familiar narrative temporality.
4. Eddington's discussion accords to the second law of thermodynamics the 'supreme position among the laws of nature'.
5. Horwich 1987: 4–11. The ten phenomena are: 'Now', 'Truth', 'Laws', 'De Facto Irreversibility', 'Knowledge', 'Causation', 'Explanation', 'Counterfactual Dependence', 'Decision' and 'Value'.

Chapter 7

Fictional Knowledge

When it comes to the internal consciousness of time, the novel picks up where philosophy leaves off. But does the novel therefore *know* something about time which is beyond the reach of philosophy? Perhaps knowledge of time is in some way the domain of philosophy, so that wherever it is that the novel goes with time, by being beyond the limits of philosophy, it cannot be an adventure in knowledge as such. There are two intimately related questions about knowledge involved in this. The first is the oldest question of all, the question of the relationship between philosophy and literature, and of the special kind of knowledge, if that is the right word, that literature might possess. The second is probably no younger, but has a more urgent contemporary application, and is the question of what use or value fictional narrative might hold for a philosophical understanding of time.

The idea that fiction might know something, perhaps something more than philosophy, has come back into focus recently in literary studies in a number of ways. An interesting case, particularly in relation to fictional knowledge, is Michael Wood's *Literature and the Taste of Knowledge* (2005). Wood's discussion of knowledge begins from Peter de Bolla's 'brilliant brief statement' of the question of knowledge in art:

> De Bolla is looking at a Barnett Newman painting (*Vir Heroicus Sublimis*) in the Museum of Modern Art in New York. He has decided that the usual critical questions – what does this painting mean?, what is it trying to say? – are the wrong ones. He offers one or two not all that appealing alternatives ('how does this painting determine my address to it?, how does it make me feel?, what does it make me feel?') and says that 'beyond these questions lies the insistent murmur of great art, the nagging thought that the work holds something to itself, contains something that, in the final analysis remains untouchable, unknowable'. Then de Bolla arrives at what I find the truly haunting question: 'What does this painting know?' (2005: 8)

This is a question that Wood wishes to put to literature rather than to painting, and to fiction in particular, and it will be a version of this question that will guide the discussion in this chapter. At the moment of posing this question, however, Wood recognises some of its implications and its dangers: the question implies that the painting might know something more than the painter, and that it might not be prepared to yield this knowledge to us; and it risks an accusation of metaphoricity, or more specifically personification, attracting the objection that a novel cannot know anything. The recognition of this danger, which seems to me to lie at the heart of a notion of fictional knowledge, is not developed by Wood at this point. In a moment reminiscent of Paul de Man's Introduction to *Allegories of Reading*, when he leaps free from the problems of linguistic reference on the grounds that its 'precise theoretical exposition' lies beyond his powers, Wood leaves the question, and the figure of speech 'to hang in the air, like an old tune, or the memory of a mood' (2005: 9). There are however some further observations to be made about the question 'What does this novel know?' One observation is that, in the transition from a painting to a novel, the question loses some of its figurative force or its metaphoricity because we are back in the domain of words. As Wood himself argues later in the work, there are many (he names seven) kinds of knowledge that can be conveyed by fictional narrative, some of which may be closely akin to what philosophy would consider to be knowledge. When a narrator or a character reflects upon a topic, or provides information, or most obviously, philosophises openly, the idea of a novel as a receptacle of knowledge looks far from implausible. Something of the force of de Bolla's question, formulated for the mute, non-verbal significance of paint, is undoubtedly lost when it is brought to bear on the novel. Another important implication of de Bolla's question which Wood does not develop is the idea that, in the comparison between philosophical and artistic knowledge it is possible that the latter will not emerge with much credit. In a scenario in which an academic contemplates a painting it is difficult to ignore the force of insult that this question can hold, and which admonishes the painting for its unsystematic and vague efforts to know (What do you know, stupid painting?). It might be argued that this is a wholly inappropriate question to ask of a painting, or a novel. There may be a kind of hostility towards art in such a question which seeks to assess its greatness in such knowledge-based terms, as if to award an honours degree classification for what it knows. Nevertheless, it is this issue of the adequation of art in terms of knowledge, the difference between philosophical and fictional knowledge, and the attribution of knowledge to a work, and not to the mind of an author or a reader, that de Bolla's question offers to Wood as a focus for the question of what a novel might know.

Support for the idea that a novel might take up where philosophy leaves off in the matter of internal time-consciousness – that it might know more about time than the philosopher – becomes easier when knowledge is thought of in this way. Questions such as 'What do novels know about time that philosophy cannot know?' or more specifically 'What does this novel know about time?' are clearly asking for some conception of knowledge which goes beyond the mere inclusion of reasoned discussion in the novel, so that something of the personification of de Bolla's question, dependent as it is on the notion of knowledge without the presence of a mind, is preserved. When Wood comes to consider the question of fictional knowledge more closely, he distinguishes, with the help of Roland Barthes, between knowing something and knowing about something. Barthes's claim, quoted by Wood, is as follows: 'The knowledge (literature) marshals is, on the other hand, never complete or final. Literature doesn't say it knows something, but that it knows *of* something; or better still it knows *about* something – that it knows about men' (2005: 38). How does this shift from *knowledge of* to *knowledge about* modify or qualify Ricoeur's position on the difference between *tales of time* and *tales about time*? Wood analyses Barthes's position in the following way:

> There is a difference, in French and in English, between knowing of and knowing about. Knowing of suggests mere acquaintance and knowing about could mean possessing substantial information. But there doesn't have to be much of a difference, and we do use the phrases as near-synonyms . . . But it's Barthes's next move that really shifts the ground . . . '*En savoir long*' is certainly different from '*en savoir*', and it is shrewd of Richard Howard (the translator) to drop the emphasis on quantity, since in English 'knowing about' can easily include the notion of knowing a great deal about . . . Literature knows a lot; it knows too much. It knows more than it wants to know, perhaps; and almost certainly more than we want it to know. This is a long way from the apparent disavowal from which the proposition started, and some considerable distance from simple knowledge by acquaintance. (2005: 39).

At first the idea of knowing something seems grander than knowing about something. This is apparent if we alter de Bolla's question 'What does this painting know?' to 'What does this painting know of?', which seems to suggest its shallowness, or 'What does this painting know about?', which seems to require a specific field of knowledge. But, according to Wood, these lesser forms of knowledge turn out to count for a great deal, so that if Barthes appeared to be describing the modesty of literature, he is in fact making quite a large claim for its epistemological function. For Wood, the displacement of 'to know of' with 'to know about' is a reinscription which elaborates on the idea of knowledge, and 'fills it with hints of unspoken knowledge' (2005: 38). In other words, the impression that knowledge about something is trivial in comparison to knowing something is mistaken, and the reinscription of the idiom restores to the idea of knowledge all of the haunting force of the unspoken which gives de Bolla's question its power. The emphasis on the unspoken is important here because it characterises a non-philosophical mode of knowledge, in which claims are implicit. But it is worth noting that the difference between the 'of' and the 'about' in this scheme cannot be aligned with Ricoeur's distinction between tales of time and tales about time, in which the force of 'of' seems to reside exactly in the implicitness of time in the tale and the force of 'about' seems to rely on some level of overt thematisation (1985: 101).

Barthes's discussion of literature and knowledge is also of interest to Wood's discussion and of use to mine for its account of the relationship between knowledge, literature and life: his claim that 'Organized or systematic knowledge is crude, life is subtle, and it is for the correction of this disparity that literature matters to us' (2005: 40). This is a statement that brings us to the second question from which we started, the question of the value of literature to a philosophical understanding of time. If we understand philosophy to be one such crude knowledge, incapable in its crude, organised ways, of understanding the subtlety of life, we find ourselves acknowledging the superiority of literature over philosophy as a form of knowledge of the world. But there is a paradox here insofar as this formula simultaneously asserts and denies the value of literature to philosophy: if literature lies in the middle between the crudity of philosophy and the subtlety of life it will be, on one hand, a more subtle form of knowledge of life than can be achieved in systematic thought and on the other, a relatively crude copy of the subtlety of life. Literature may provide, for example, a case study in internal time-consciousness, but philosophy would be better to deal directly with life itself, where the full subtlety of internal time-consciousness can be encountered undistorted by the demands of verbal representation. The value of literature to philosophy depends upon whether we view literature as the subject or the object of knowledge, that is, as a form of knowledge of life, or as an object which knowledge might try to understand or describe, the knower or the known. Let us suppose for a moment that the novel is superior to philosophy when it comes to knowledge of internal time-consciousness, that it can capture something which escapes systematic knowledge, or that it takes up where philosophy leaves off. The disparity between the knowing subject (the novel) and the object known (interiority) is not so great, according to Barthes's view, as that between philosophy and the mind. How then are we to know what it is that the novel knows about internal time-consciousness? In order to draw the novel's knowledge of life into the light, or to return to Wood's metaphor, in order to give voice to the unspoken knowledge that the novel possesses about time, we require a discourse about literature, or a knowledge of literature. Whether we call this knowledge philosophy, criticism or theory, the gap between this organised and systematic knowledge and the subtlety of life is encountered again in the gap between systematic knowledge and literature. Presumably, however, the gap is less wide, so that knowledge of literature will take us some way towards knowledge of life. And this, for Barthes, is why literature matters to us: it is a stepping stone by way of which philosophy can reach out towards a comprehension of life's subtleties.

Though it may be music to the ears of creative writing students everywhere, this model of the relationship between philosophical knowledge of time and fictional knowledge of time is problematic in many ways, many of which are concerned with the ambiguities of the concept of knowledge itself, and the difficulties of viewing representation as a form of knowledge. Nor is the tension between philosophical and fictional knowledge of time in any way new, dominating as it has the critical and philosophical engagement with Proust and the analysis of *Mrs Dalloway*. I would like to address these old questions to more recent novels, to Ali Smith's *The Accidental* and Ian McEwan's *Saturday*, which serve as interesting examples in which the problems of knowledge, fictional knowledge of internal time-consciousness, and critical knowledge of this fictional knowledge, interact with each other.

Accidental Knowledge

What then does Ali Smith's *The Accidental* know about time? In many ways this is a more focused question than 'Is this a novel about time?', and one which avoids the absurdities of Ricoeur's discussion as he tries to weigh various topics against each other in his critical quest for what is principally at issue. It may be that some of the metaphysical baggage which comes with the idea of knowledge is unwanted or unnecessary, but this is also the question's strength, in that it deals head on with the question of what the novel knows about life, and how this relates to the knowledge of life that can be claimed in philosophy. In the first place, *The Accidental* has a certain amount of explicit thematisation, and even discussion of time, which takes place in the mind of Astrid, a twelve-year-old girl who is on holiday with her family in Norfolk. The novel's focalisation rotates around the four members of the family, so that the inner lives of Astrid's brother Magnus, her father Michael and her mother Eve are available to us in turn. When we first meet Astrid, she is contemplating beginnings:

> Because why do people always say the day starts now? Really it starts in the middle of the night at a fraction of a second past midnight. But it's not supposed to have begun until the dawn, really the dark is still last night and it isn't morning till the light, though actually it is morning as soon as it was a fraction of a second past twelve i.e. that experiment where you divide something down and down like the distance between the ground and a ball that's been bounced on it so that it can be proved, Magnus says, that the ball never actually touches the ground. Which is junk because of course it touches the ground otherwise how would it bounce, it wouldn't have anything to bounce off, but it can actually be proved by science that it doesn't. (2005: 7)

Astrid might well have been reading Book XI of Augustine's *Confessions* and the contemplation of daybreak which was discussed in Chapter 4 of this book, and on which Augustine bases his whole problem of the vanishing present. But Astrid's interest in dawn is more complex and more cluttered than Augustine's, since it is not only a question about the divisibility of a moment which is at stake, but also a tension between the moment of dawn and the moment officially known as the start of morning by clock time. Astrid's mind jumps to the problem of the divisibility of the present for good reason, since it affects both these conceptions of morning, and so to the idea that the systematic knowledge of science will be of no assistance in this, since it will only prove to her something that she knows is not true. If Astrid has already gone some way beyond Augustine in her contemplation of daybreak, the effect is about to be compounded, because Astrid lives in the age of the digital video camera, and she is taping dawns:

> She now has nine dawns one after the other on the mini dv tape in her Sony digital. Thursday 10 July 2003, Friday 11 July 2003, Saturday 12, Sunday 13, Monday 14, Tuesday 15, Wednesday 16, Thursday 17 and today Friday 18. But it is hard to know what moment exactly dawn is. All there is when you look at it on the camera screen is the view of outside getting more visible. So does it mean that the beginning is something to do with being able to see? That the day begins as soon as you wake up and open your eyes? So when Magnus finally wakes up in the afternoon and they can hear him moving about in the room that's his in this dump of a substandard house, does that mean that the day is still beginning? Is the beginning different for everyone? Or do beginnings just keep stretching on forwards and forwards all day? Or maybe it is back and back they stretch. Because every time you open your eyes there was a time before that when you closed them then a different time before that when you opened them, all the way back, through all the sleeping and the

waking and the ordinary things like blinking, to the first time you ever open your eyes, which is probably round about the moment you are born. (2005: 8)

Astrid's question here about the connection between beginnings and vision, and her subsequent thoughts about when Magnus's day begins, and the beginnings which occur every time she blinks, establish a dichotomy between the personal vision of the eye and the apparently collective vision of the camera which runs through the novel as a whole. It is part of a dialectic between private subjectivity and the shared history of cinema, and more generally between subjective and objective time. The question also contains a clear echo of Augustine's efforts to hold the vision of daybreak before the mind's eye, for the purposes of foretelling the future from the present:

> Suppose that I am watching the break of day. I predict that the sun is about to rise. What I see is present but what I foretell is future. I do not mean that the sun is future, for it already exists, but that its rise is future, because it has not yet happened. But I could not foretell the sunrise unless I had a picture of it in my mind, just as I have at this moment while I am speaking about it. Yet the dawn, which I see in the sky, is not the sunrise, which is future. The future, then, is not yet; it is not at all, it cannot possibly be seen. But it can be foretold from things which are present, because they exist now and can therefore be seen. (Augustine 1967: 268)

For Astrid, there is the moment of daybreak and then there is the moment of watching the recording of daybreak, and whereas in the former, sunrise is in the future, and so has not happened yet, in the latter, the future has already happened, and can be quickly accessed. The camera is deeply bound up with anticipations of the future, and particularly with the anticipation of retrospect, for Astrid. She films things imagining or hoping that her recordings will become significant archive in the future, that the police will come looking for her because 'someone in authority will remember and say oh that twelve-year-old girl was there with a camera, maybe she recorded something really what is the word crucial to our investigations' (2005: 10) or that her most mundane actions will become cultural history:

> There are two ways to watch what you are filming: 1. on the little screen and 2. through the viewer. Real filmmakers always use the viewer though it is harder to see with it. She puts her eye to the viewer and records her hand making the latch go up then down. In a hundred years' time these latches may not exist any more and this film will be proof that they did and will act as evidence for people who need to know in the future how latches like this one worked. (2005: 15)

The implication here is that the camera is her future, in the sense that she will be a real filmmaker, but also that her personal actions will be valuable archive, that the things of the present have a built-in obsolescence, and so are already the objects of historical curiosity. The camera is not only the focus of Astrid's Augustinian puzzles about time, but the technological version of the traditional diary and all of its most traditional functions in the emergence and development of self-consciousness. It is a diary with a firm emphasis on the future, which provides Astrid with the most complex ways of envisaging retrospect as well as the most straightforward ways of measuring time: 'By the end of their time here she will have sixty-one beginnings, depending on if they go home on the Friday, the Saturday or the Sunday. Sixty-one minus nine, i.e. still at least fifty- two more to go' (2005: 13).

There are two kinds of time-consciousness at work in Astrid's character, one of which is an explicit interest in time and beginnings as manifested in her opening discussions of time, and the other of which occurs at a less conscious level and which demonstrates the importance of time to her thought in more implicit and less philosophical ways. Her interest in digital video archiving spans both modes of time-consciousness in the sense that it is the object and means of her reflection, as well as a pervasive influence on her awareness of the world in general. She is, for example, highly aware of CCTV, and of its relation to time, its ironies and its inherent power relations, to the point where she films the CCTV cameras which are filming her in Norwich station, and is asked to stop on the grounds that she is recording the details of the security system. She is preoccupied with the time recorded by CCTV cameras in which nothing happens, and this leads her into a contemplation of time without happenings. Having counted out a minute on her watch in which 'not a single thing happens', Astrid comes to consider the events of this apparently empty minute:

> It is actually not true that not a single thing happened in that minute she counted out just now. There were the birds and things like insects flying. Crows or something probably cawed in the heat above her. They are doing it now. There is the tall white plant over behind the wall, cow something it is called. In sixty seconds it probably moved a bit in the air and it must even have grown but in a way that can't be seen by the human eye. (2005: 127)

In her discussion of beginnings, in her obsession with CCTV, in her preoccupation with digital video, and here above, as she contemplates the things which escape the notice of the human eye, Astrid's time-consciousness is highly visual in its nature, and her mind style is one which consciously reflects upon and unconsciously enacts this relation between time and vision. This extends to her interest in colour, which again becomes entangled in her consciousness of time:

> Astrid had never really noticed how green things are before. Even the stone is green. The door of the locked church door is brown-green, has a sheen of green on it from it just being there in the weather etc. It is a really bright colour. If she had her camera she would have just filmed the colour for a whole minute and then later she would be able to see what it really looks like, that colour. (2005, 127)

The conscious time-consciousness involved here is in a running theme about the measurement of time, and the importance of a single minute, while the less conscious time-consciousness is the temporal structure which is at work in her relation with her camera, whereby the reality of something before the eye can only be encountered in retrospect as its recording. The first kind of time-consciousness is most obviously manifested in Astrid's constant calculations and measurement, for example, in her interest in people's ages, and her habit of translating these ages into proportions of old and new based on the length of time each person has lived in the new century in relation to the old. The second kind of time-consciousness is derived in a more obvious way from her own age and her position in history at that age, and represents something distinctly modern about the portrait. At both levels, the accumulated effect of the association between time and vision is an account of her time-consciousness which goes far beyond the mere relation of what Astrid thinks about time in her more philosophical moments. Her thoughts about time are embedded in her general mind style, in the language that she overuses, in the repetition of her ideas, and in a set of modern conditions in which time is encountered. '5.16am on the substandard clock radio' (10) : a phrase as simple as this plays its part in the knowledge that the novel builds up of Astrid's experience of time, containing as it does a marker of her mind style in the word 'substandard', which she applies to everything, her preoccupation with daybreak, and even the set of conditions for the technological measurement and recording of time in relation to which this clock radio is judged. The substandard clock radio is *Mrs Dalloway*'s Big Ben, interrupting the flow of Astrid's subjectivity to remind us of the world which is collective and shared.

If we go back to the beginning, or to Astrid's contemplation of beginnings, it is clear that a straightforward comparison between Astrid and Augustine will miss the point when it comes to the question of philosophical and fictional knowledge. I have already argued this point the other way around, by claiming that the full interest of Augustine's discussion of time is only realised by the reader who does not, as most philosophers have done, isolate the discussion of time from the narrative as a whole. Even if Astrid gives Augustine a run for his money in the discussion of dawn, this is not the way that fictional and philosophical knowledge can be compared. The most important aspect of Astrid's discussion of beginnings is one that we have not discussed yet, namely the fact that it is itself a beginning. This is not to say that openings which know that they are openings are in any way of value in themselves, or to be admired on account of their self-consciousness. The novel in the act of self-contemplation, contemplating the idea of beginnings at the beginning and of endings at the end, is rivalled only by the self-conscious poststructuralist preface at the outset of a work of literary theory for the status of the contemporary world's worst cliché. But this is not what we have in Astrid's concern with beginnings, nor with the novel's interest in its own structural principles and stages more generally. *The Accidental* is a novel which begins five times, and then has five middles, which are followed by five endings. In each case, four of the five sections are accounted for by the four main characters, Astrid, Magnus, Eve and Michael, while the fifth is the voice of Alhambra, or Amber, named after the cinema in which she was conceived. The connection between Alhambra and Amber should not be oversimplified, and is explored below in more detail, but the starting point here is that Amber 'is' Alhambra, the narrator of these peripheral sections of the novel. Amber's narratives differ from those of the Smart family: whereas Astrid, Magnus, Eve and Michael are focalised in a number of ways by a third person narrator, Amber's discourses are in the first person. As well as being considerably shorter than the other sections, these discourses, largely because of the absence of the third-person voice, adopt a different attitude to fictional time, one which is external to the narrated events of the novel, and which rushes through time in truncated autobiographical sweeps. That Amber is in some way external to time is something that the novel continually suggests. She wears a watch which is stopped at 7 o'clock, so that when time is passing for Magnus, it is static for Amber (144). Her name, in the playfully associative mind of Michael's sonnet sequence, is 'an exotic fixative. Amber preserved things that weren't meant to last. Amber gave dead things a chance to live forever' (163). This externality to time is literalised by the externality of her short first-person narratives to the three sections of the novel, which are named, in the same spirit of literality as 'The Beginning', 'The Middle' and 'The End'. As we have already seen, 'The Beginning' is more than just a literal self-designation – it is a topic which lies at the heart of Astrid's interest in time – and nor is it a single point of origin, as Astrid's dawns and her blinkings of the eye make clear. The multiplicity of beginnings is inherent in the narrative's structure, which begins again with each character's focalisation, and begins again not only at the beginning, but also at the middle and at the end. The ability of the beginning to operate in this way as structural self-designation, as a structural feature, as a thematic concern, and as a preoccupation of characters is itself literalised in a kind of graphic joke, in which the three titles simultaneously name their sections of the novel and become the first words of the focalised discourse of each character, so stepping across the ontological boundary between real and fictional time. This is a literalisation of a relationship between the outside and the inside of fiction, and I use the word literal here in its literal sense, to mean that it pertains to letters on a page.[1]

Amber's externality to time, like the word 'beginning', has a graphic dimension. It is Amber's words which begin the book, and they come before the beginning, and before the words 'The Beginning'. She begins, in the first section with the words 'My mother began me . . .' and in the other sections with 'I was born . . .', 'I am born . . .' and 'I was born'. She is a framing device for the novel as a whole and for each of its sections as well as being dramatised within each section, and as such she is, in Derrida's words, 'invagination', or 'an internal pocket which is larger than the whole' (1992a: 228). It would be more accurate, then, to say that Amber is outside and within time, and her autobiographical descriptions seem to confirm this. She may have a mother and a father, but her parentage oscillates ambiguously between real people and characters in films which played in the Alhambra cinema where, one infers with some difficulty, her real father worked as the manager. Cinema begat her: 'My father was Terence and my mother was Julie. (Stamp. Christie) I was born and bred in the hills (alive) and the animals (talked to)' (105). This sense of cinema as parentage is established by a set of references to films, featuring Terence Stamp and Julie Christie, which were part of the actual environment of the Alhambra cinema, as well as a more metaphorical and symbolic environment which begat Amber. The more associative references which evoke Dr Doolittle and the Von Trapp family, as a shared history, and the blurring of real and symbolic conditions, of characters and actors, are neither accidental nor trivial. They are part of the general soup of historical and cinematic influences which Amber, or Alhambra, who is both an exotic fixative and a cinema, invokes:

> I was formed and made in the Saigon days, the Rhodesian days, the days of the rivers of blood. DISEMBOWEL ENOCH POWELL. Apollo 7 splashdowned. Tunbridge Wells was flooded. A crowd flowed over London Bridge, and thirty-six Americans made bids to buy it. They shot the king in Memphis, which delayed the Academy Awards telecast for two whole days.

He had a dream, he held these truths to be self-evident, that all men were created equal and would one day sit down together at the table of brother-hood. They shot the other brother at the Ambassador Hotel. RIGHTEOUS BROS it said in lights above the hotel car park. Meanwhile my father was a watchmaker and my mother could fly using only an umbrella. When I was a child I ran the Grand National on my horse. They didn't know I was a girl until I fainted and they unbuttoned my jockey shirt. But anything was pos-sible. We had a flying floating car. We stopped the rail disaster by waving our petticoats at the train; my father was innocent in prison, my mother made ends meet. I sold flowers in Covent Garden. A posh geezer taught me how to speak proper and took me to the races, designed by Cecil Beaton, though they dubbed my voice in the end because the singing wasn't good enough. (2005: 104).

The first-person pronoun is under some stress here as it strains to encom-pass cinematic history (actors) and cinematic narratives (characters) within the I of self-narration. But the disdain for that ontological bound-ary is subsumed in the more general relationship between cinematic and socio-political history. These are Amber's multiplicitous beginnings, and they assign to her the narrative function of representing a collective history of representations, which encompass the private reflections of the novel's other characters as history encompasses the individual. Like Rushdie's Saleem Sinai, she is the personification of a babble of repre-sented voices against which the personal lives of Astrid, Magnus, Eve and Michael are particular and parochial. The connection with Rushdie here is worth contemplating, partly for the dialogue it creates with another novel preoccupied with beginnings, both of a fictional and of a socio-political nature. Both *The Accidental* and *Midnight's Children* borrow their joke about beginnings from Sterne's *Tristram Shandy*, in which the conditions of Tristram's conception, and therefore the narra-tion of those conditions, play a prominent part. The conception and birth of Tristram Shandy and Saleem Sinai provide a backdrop in clock time, or in historical time, against which the digressions of narrative time take place, but in the case of *The Accidental* and *Midnight's Children*, the personification of history in Amber and Saleem ensures that, in the opposition between the individual and history, or the per-sonal and the collective, the subset contains the universal set, or the part contains the whole. The idea of a person as a part of a social or histor-ical totality is the basis of time structure in many novels, whether it is through the interaction of the individual with history in the historical novel, or the tension between the temporality of the inner life and the measurement of clock time in the outside world. By putting historical time inside the individual, these novels disturb the ordinary conception of time that we find, for example, in *Mrs Dalloway*, or in *Ulysses*, in which the order of the outside and the chaos of interiority happily co-exist, or in which the individual exists within history. We find here something of the logic of Hegel's 'concrete universal', or the paradox of the immanent or embodied universal according to which a particularity can represent a totality, or a part can stand for the whole. This may be more obviously a conscious game in *Midnight's Children*, with its many literalisations of ideas of fragmentation and unity. The perforated sheet, for example, through which Adam Aziz becomes acquainted with his future wife, assembling a picture of her as a totality bit by bit, is itself a parody of the efforts of Adela Quested in Forster's *A Passage to India* to find in any tiny detail an emblem of Indian-ness in general. The idea of embodied totality, or of the relationship between the particular person and their representative function is similarly literalised in the relationship between Amber and Alhambra, where the former is within time and the latter outside of time. This reading of Amber, as the personification of cinema and of history on the outside, and her interactions with Astrid in all of her particularity, is corroborated by the extract from John Berger which begins the novel, before the beginning: 'Between the experience of living a normal life at this moment on the planet and the public narratives being offered to give a sense to that life, the empty space, the gap, is enormous'.

Just as the word 'beginning' traverses from one order of reality to another, so too does Amber cross the boundary from the outside of fictional time to the inside, carrying all of her overtly symbolic functions with her into the realm of the particular. For all that Alhambra represents about time, as Amber, she is capable of interaction with Astrid in the mundane realm of particularity that is the Smarts' family holiday in Norfolk. The intervention narrated by *The Accidental* is partly this metaleptic intervention of the symbolic into the particular, and this is the source of Amber's atmosphere of other-worldliness, of significance, and of power. The embodied interaction which takes place as a result of this intervention, such as the interaction between Amber and Astrid, is characterised by an oscillation between particular and universal significance, and at times has the character of a post-symbolic commentary on the relationship between the symbolic and the particular itself. The interaction between Amber and Astrid is, among many other things, an encounter between two very different relations to time, and one facet of this difference is the relationship between cinema and digital video. Though Amber has no real connection with cinema within the Norfolk narrative, in her relation to her metaleptic other she is the embodiment of cinema, its offspring, and its history. How then are we to read the key event in this relationship, when Amber drops

Astrid's video camera from the pedestrian bridge and they watch it smash into fragments below:

> Halfway across the pedestrian bridge, above the roaring traffic, Amber stops. They lean over and look at the view and the countryside again. It is beautiful. It is really English and quintessential. They watch the cars beneath them going in and coming out, moving like a two-way river. The sunlight off the windscreens and the paint of the cars is flashy in Astrid's eyes. It is easier to look at the further-away cars fading into a see-through wall of more shimmering heat. Their colours melt through it as if cars aren't made of anything solid.
>
> It is a beautiful summer afternoon, like the perpetual summers used to be in the old days, before Astrid was born.
>
> Then Amber drops the camera over the side of the bridge.
>
> Astrid watches as it falls through the air. She hears her own voice remote and faraway, then she hears the plastic-sounding noise of her camera as it hits the tarmac. It sounds so small. She sees the truck wheel hit it and send it spinning under the wheels of the car behind it on the inside lane, breaking it into small pieces which scatter it all over the road. Other cars come behind and carry on hitting the pieces, running them over, bouncing them across the road surface. (2005: 118)

If Amber is a symbolic mother to Astrid, this episode is where the symbolic mother displaces the real mother. The camera, as a birthday present from her mother, is an emblem of her beginnings, as well as being the archiving machine on which Astrid has recorded all her subsequent beginnings, that is until Amber arrived, when she stopped recording dawns. The displacement of the real by the symbolic mother is strengthened by the echo of Eve's own language in Astrid's perception of the scene which precedes the smashing of the camera. The countryside is 'English and quintessential', an idiom that we know belongs to Eve from the novel's start.[2] The beauty of the afternoon evokes in Astrid's mind the perpetual summers of the old days, before Astrid was born, and again we hear the echo of her mother's nostalgia for the days before Astrid was begun.[3] Eve, as her name suggests, has a fundamentally Adamic view of time (Astrid's biological father is called Adam) as a fall from Eden, and she is imaged as mother nature at the same time as she is established as Astrid's natural mother: she is her literal and her symbolic beginnings, the mother of Astrid and the mother of all women. Both Eve and Amber then have symbolic maternal relations to Astrid, and both entail the positioning of the mother before the beginning of Astrid, literally, symbolically, and in Amber's case in terms of the novel itself, which she begins before Astrid. If we think about this in relation to Amber's own peculiar account of her parentage, of her parents as actors and actresses, as films, as cinema workers, and as cinema itself, we are drawn to a reading of this scene which places Eve's Adamic myth, of nostalgia for the perpetual summers of old, in competition with Amber's, which views (quite literally) the digital video camera as a fall (also literally) from the Golden Age of cinema. By smashing the camera, the symbolic mother displaces the mother, and the Adamic myth of a lost Eden is transformed into a nostalgia for the camera's own cinematic parentage.

In a novel called *The Accidental*, we might not expect everything to be intended, but there is a strong feeling in this scene, and in the novel as a whole, that the novel knows what it knows about time. It is no accident that the road in this scene is a 'two-way river' above which Amber and Astrid are poised. If time is a river, this looks like a multiply suggestive symbol: it is the violation of the pastoral scene, but it is also a kind of encoding of time, perhaps two different attitudes to time, or more plausibly still, an encoding of middleness. The second section of the novel, 'The Middle', has begun a few pages before this scene, and begun with the same traversal of the boundary between the form and content of the novel: 'The Middle . . . of the dual carriage way . . .' (108–9). In the first crossing of the road, which was not by the bridge, but involved stopping the cars, the symbolism is explicit:

> It is insane. It is really dangerous. It is a bit like the story from the bible when the sea parts in two, except it is traffic. It is like Amber is blessed with a magnetic forcefield from outer space or another galaxy. (109)

In both of these crossings, Amber's superheroic power and her otherworldliness are entwined with her metaleptic crossings between the middle as a structural principle for the novel, and the middle as a literal position within the frame of the fiction. The interpretation of this scene as a symbolic encounter between digital video and cinema depends on the metaleptic travel involved in Amber's duality as an internal dramatisation in the story and as an external frame narrator, since it invokes symbolic associations established outside of the spatiotemporal frame represented by the holiday in Norfolk. But the middleness of Amber and Astrid here is part of the way that the novel gives the impression of knowing itself, of knowing what it knows about time, since it reinforces the co-presence of fictional and textual time. It is no accident that Astrid and Amber are in the middle of the bridge here, and that the road is a perpendicular axis on which they are in the middle. In the middle of their crossing, they are at the centre of a cross. To borrow a bad joke from Barbara Johnson, they are a kind of cruci-fiction, a crossing point between the book itself and its fictional frame (Johnson 1980). One of these axes signifies their position in the middle of the book, with fictional time still to come and fictional time under the bridge. The present itself is difficult to grasp. It is easier for Astrid to look at the further away cars, as they fade into a see-through wall of shimmering heat, than to look at the cars beneath. In the intensity of the moment, Astrid hears her own voice, remote and far away, as if the moment is structured as self-distance, or as if her own experience of this central moment parallels that of the novel, as it tells its story and at the same time knows itself from a distance.

The accidental and the intentional intersect here in a complex way with the question of fictional knowledge. Let me return to Michael Wood's discussion for some accidental help on the question of knowledge:

> It is no accident that – this is the phrase writers always use when they are about to do something slippery with their argument. Let me start again. It is not, I hope, merely a piece of free association on my part that brings together Barthes's idea that literature makes knowledge into a holiday and Ludwig Wittgenstein's image for the occasions when philosophical problems arise: when language goes on holiday. (2005: 42)

It is an accident that Wood should make this observation about the argumentative idiom 'it is no accident' in the context of a discussion of knowledge as a holiday, and that I should be writing about knowledge in relation to a novel about a holiday. It is an accident that Barthes's notion that literature makes knowledge a holiday, and Wittgenstein's remark that philosophical problems arise when language goes on holiday seem to relate so well to *The Accidental*. But it is no accident that I have been using the idiom heavily over the previous paragraphs, because the question of knowledge, of what this novel knows about time, is necessarily connected to the question of who it is that is doing the knowing. As Wood's warning at the outset of the chapter makes clear, one of the possible objections to de Bolla's question about what a painting knows is that it personifies the painting, though one could counter-object that it is only when knowledge is thought of as the exclusive activity of a conscious mind that this can be seen as personification at all. Whereas in the first section of 'The beginning' knowledge about time can be attributed to Astrid herself, the interaction of Astrid and Amber, and so of their ideas about time, attributes knowledge to another level of discourse: not to the mind of a fictional character but to the mind which orchestrates their interaction. In the camera-smashing scene, knowledge of time is produced partly by this interaction, and partly by the organisation of a symbolic system, in which a complex set of ideas about time can be said to be encoded. This is a novel, I have claimed, which knows what it knows about time, in the sense that it seems to contain a substantial and complex body of ideas which pertain to time as a topic and at the same time recognise the metaleptic parallel entailed in the relation between the topic of time and the temporal logic of narrative. It is not only in the interaction of Amber and Astrid, then, that knowledge of time is produced, but in the interaction between the topic of time and the temporal logic of narrative fiction, where these two interactions are unified by the duality of Amber's ontological frame. Can we then speak of the novel's knowledge of time without assigning this knowledge to the author, or claiming the intentional nature of its knowledge as a kind of conscious encoding in fictional form? Is this knowledge of time meant, and if not, does it qualify as knowledge? 'Believe me. Everything is meant' Alhambra declares after the announcement of her own name at the start of the novel. This guarantee of intention serves as a commentary on the novel's symbolism in general and seems to assign an authorial intention to Alhambra herself, though she is not an author. An atmosphere of authorial surrogacy surrounds Alhambra and Amber throughout the narrative, not only in her power, in the idea of her symbolic motherhood of Astrid, in her position as the narrative frame and her un-timeliness, but in a kind of knowingness. Here again the mirroring of Amber and Eve is apparent, since Eve is also an author, married to an academic reader, and destined at the end of the novel to become Amber, or to step into her role as the stranger who intervenes in the life of a family. If we are to understand Amber as a surrogate author, her metaleptic correspondences do not stop at the boundary between Alhambra's symbolic function and the inner fictional frame: they extend outwards to the amber cover (the original hardback cover), to the author, and the novel's title. And this will suffice, at least, as a way of understanding, with the help of the novel's implicit self-commentary, the mode of knowledge that we might expect from a novel about time: that it might fall somewhere between the intentional conduct of an enquiry and the generation of accidental insights.

If Astrid represents a combination of conscious and unconscious forms of time-consciousness, so too, it might be said, does the novel as a whole, and what *The Accidental* knows about time has to be understood as the sum of the two. This is the only way that de Bolla's attribution of knowledge to the painting rather than the painter can be observed in relation to the novel. Just as Umberto Eco attributes the idea of intention to the literary work, rather than the literary artist, in the notion of Intentio Operis,[4] so too can the attribution of knowledge in a novel free itself from the limits of authorial consciousness. Fictional knowledge in this light becomes a combination of blindness and insight, in de Man's terminology, so that sometimes what a novel knows might be inherent in what it doesn't know, or generated in the interaction between its conscious projects and its accidental effects. Nor will a novel's efforts to know what it knows, or to be in possession of its own blind spots, alter this model of knowledge in any fundamental way, since its efforts will only ever specify the distance between its self-knowledge and the knowledge of a given reader. When the model of cognition is one in which the work of art contains 'hints of unspoken knowledge', knowledge will necessarily lie beyond reach, and so remain inaccessible to the reader. In this respect the de Bolla–Wood question seems to lag behind a considerable quantity of theory in deconstruction and psychoanalysis which takes the inaccessibility of fictional knowledge as a starting point, and yet which seems to express itself in very similar terms to de Bolla's original question. In Derrida's *Given Time*, for example, the notion of the true secret, or the secret which cannot be revealed, is central to an understanding of the operations of fiction. There is, as Hillis Miller puts it, an 'essential relation between literature and the secret':

> Literature keeps its secret. A work of literature is all on the surface, all there in the words on the page, imprinted on a surface that cannot be gone behind. This means that there are certain secrets or enigmas in a work of literature that cannot by any means be penetrated, though answers to the questions they pose may be essential to a reading of the work. (2001: 152)

This notion, that a work of literature is all on the surface, is a useful link between the domain of art and that of fiction, reminding us that the insistent murmur of great art, the untouchable and unknowable secret that a work keeps to itself, is at work in verbal as well as visual art, however cluttered the notion of words may be with imputations of deeper consciousness. But it is also an indication that the problem of fictional knowledge is at a rather busy intersection of contemporary thinking: it is Derrida's call of the Other, Badiou's unnameable, de Man's blindness, Lyotard's inexpressible, Beckett's ineffable, Freud's uncanny, Lacan's real, Conrad's secret and, for Wittgenstein, what lies beyond the limits of language. Must we then settle for the paradox from which we began, of unknowable knowledge, or that fiction might know, perhaps better than philosophy does, that time is unknowably complex? The remainder of this chapter is concerned to show that the way out of this paradox, or the way into another one, is through a refurbishment of the model of knowledge on which it rests.

Fictions of Today

Wood describes his project in *Literature and the Taste of Knowledge* as an attempt to describe 'what particular forms of knowledge in literature may look like, or taste like' (2005: 11). It is, he claims, only going to be a taste. The main course lies elsewhere. If as Barthes claims organised knowledge is crude and life is subtle with literature in between, our options look unpromising. Life itself surely cannot be the main course. To claim that life knows about life is like claiming that space knows about astronomy: it removes the foundational relation of knowledge between the knower and the known. The other direction isn't much more promising, since it offers only a crude reduction of the thing to be known, even if it preserves the analytical distance, the doubleness of the relation between the knower and the known, which the self-knowing universe lacks. Barthes's claim is of course an unsupportable slander upon the value of organised knowledge, and if philosophy is to be counted as a form of organised knowledge, a slander upon the value of philosophy. Of course, life can be crude and philosophy subtle; life can be full of knowledge and philosophy can be disorganised; and philosophy is a part of life as much as life is a part of philosophy. Nevertheless, the sense of a gap between knowledge and life is at the heart of Wood's enquiry: 'between what can be said and what can't; of what takes the place of thinking when we encounter or engineer the unthinkable' (11).

This gap between knowledge and life, and the place of literature in this gap, is also at the heart of Ian McEwan's *Saturday*, insofar as its protagonist, Henry Perowne, whose inner life the novel explores, is a man of science. He is a neurosurgeon with an uneasy attitude to literature, who cannot quite accept the importance of fiction as a form of knowledge. He wants the world to be explained, not reinvented, and has no wish to be a 'spectator of other lives, of imaginary lives' (2005: 66). The first effect of this is irony, since Perowne's world is a reinvented one, and his life is imaginary. The novel therefore stages a contest between scientific and literary knowledge but one which is circumscribed by the difference between what he knows and what we know, namely that he is fictional. But where a metafictional novel would incorporate this knowledge into the novel itself, so claiming it as its own, as self-knowledge, *Saturday* is vigilant in the preservation of its realistic frame. This realism, and its rigorous referential illusion, is a doubling of the irony, because it is part of the discussion about literature which is dramatised in Perowne's relationship with his daughter Daisy. Though he distrusts literature generally, his fictional preferences are for the realism of *Anna Karenina* and *Madame Bovary*:

They had the virtue at least of representing a recognisable physical reality, which could not be said for the so-called magical realists she opted to study in her final year. What were these authors of reputation doing – grown men and women of the twentieth century – granting supernatural powers to their characters? He never made it all the way through a single one of those irksome confections. And written for adults, not children. In more than one, heroes or heroines were born with or sprouted wings, a symbol, in Daisy's terms, of their liminality; naturally, learning to fly became a metaphor for bold aspiration. Others were granted a magical sense of smell, or tumbled unharmed out of high-flying aircraft. One visionary saw through a pub window his parents as they had been some weeks after his conception, discussing the possibility of aborting him. (2005: 67)

The distaste for the supernatural is part of Perowne's scientific mindset, and extends to a suspicion towards symbolism as well as an outright rejection of experiments with time. 'You ninny. You Gradgrind', Daisy reproves him. 'It's literature, not physics!' (68). It could be said then that Perowne would approve of the kind of novel he is in, with its strict observation of the linearity of time and its recognisable physical reality, except that he fails to see the point of those either:

> What did he grasp after all? That adultery is understandable but wrong, that nineteenth-century women had a hard time of it, that Moscow and the Russian countryside and provincial France were once just so. If, as Daisy said, the genius was in the detail, then he was unmoved. The details were apt and convincing enough, but surely not so very difficult to marshal if you were halfway observant and had the patience to write them all down. (67)

In answer to the question of what novels know, Perowne would say 'nothing', since they are divided between childish make-believe, pointless reinvention, inane moral teachings and workmanlike drudgery. The knowledge of the neurosurgeon is, by contrast, a thing of beauty:

> To go right in through the face, remove the tumour through the nose, to deliver the patient back into her life, without pain or infection, with her vision restored was a miracle of human ingenuity. Almost a century of failure and partial success lay behind this one procedure, of other routes tried and rejected, and decades of fresh invention to make it possible, including the microscope and the fibre optic lighting. The procedure was humane and daring – the spirit of benevolence enlivened by the boldness of a high-wire circus act. (44–5)

This instrumental rationale for the value of scientific knowledge underlies much of Perowne's thinking, which celebrates the contemporary world for its 'wondrous machines', and views the city itself as a 'brilliant success, a biological masterpiece' of technological achievement. The opposition of literature and scientific knowledge is therefore partly acted out in the relationship between Perowne and the literary members of his family, in the figures of Daisy and his father-in-law Grammaticus, who are poets. But there is a less obvious way in which this opposition is developed, which lies, once again, in the relationship between the apparent reality of Perowne as the protagonist of a realistic novel and his fictionality. *Saturday* pitches a neurosurgeon's notion of interiority against the novelist's, and this contest is conducted not only between the different notions of knowledge held by its characters, but in the relationship between the central character and the novel itself. Hence, on one hand, there is a notion of the mind as pure matter:

> A man who attempts to ease the miseries of failing minds by repairing brains is bound to respect the material world, its limits, and what it can sustain – consciousness, no less . . . he knows it for a quotidian fact, the mind is what the brain, mere matter, performs. (67)

On the other hand the mind which thinks this, and everything else that it thinks on a single day, Saturday, 15 February 2003, is the subject of McEwan's novel, so that the conception of the mind as matter is also the matter of the novel's exploration of interiority. Perowne is both a subject and an object of knowledge, but of course he doesn't know it. He is the object of knowledge because an omniscient narrator is allowing us access to his head, and this access therefore provides an ironic contrast with the kind of access to heads which is the stuff of neurosurgery.

The idea of omniscience is interesting, for obvious reasons, for a consideration of knowledge. Perowne, thought of as a person, may have views about literature, and about its inferiority to science, but his own knowledge is deficient to the extent that the real debate between scientific and fictional knowledge is being conducted at a level to which he has no access. He is watched or known from above, as it were, and this omniscient knowledge of him is by far the most important thing that he doesn't know. His own condition as a fictional narrative is unknowable to him, and it could be argued unknowable to the omniscient narrative voice itself, which is concerned with knowing him, but not with its own relation to that knowledge. The omniscient narration may then know everything about Perowne, but like Perowne, there are some important things that it doesn't seem to know about itself, such as the fact that it is engaged in a polemic between literature and science. And what kind of omniscience is it, we might ask, that doesn't know everything about itself? Nicholas Royle has raised similar questions in relation to the idea of omniscience in *The Uncanny*. 'Omniscience', he argues, is simply the wrong word for this basic predicament in fictional narrative, not only because it carries within it a specifically Christian ambience in which Christian subjects are the objects of knowledge to an all-knowing god, but also because it is simply misleading. If omniscience is normally thought of as 'access to consciousness' it is, Royle argues, also access to unconsciousness, or to what a character does not think and know. Omniscience, Royle argues, 'became a widespread literary critical term just as psychoanalysis was establishing the structural and conditioning impossibility of complete knowledge of one's own thoughts and feelings, let alone complete knowledge of anyone else's' (2003: 261):

> reliance on the term 'omniscience' thus acts as a means by which criticism can avoid the obligation to reflect more rigorously on what psychoanalysis might have to say about unconscious knowledge and desire, or, conversely, what literary fiction may have to say about psychoanalysis. (260–1)

Certainly the idea of access to Perowne's interiority only seems to raise questions about what he does not know, and indeed seems to locate the novel's knowledge in a kind of structural tension between the knower and the known. Like Miller, Royle resorts to Derrida's notion of the secret as literature's essential characteristic, as a means of approaching the structural and conditioning impossibility of complete self-knowledge which is at work in this relation between a character and the so-called omniscience of the narration in which that character is represented – the 'telepathic bonds and connections at the most decisive and elementary structural level, between narrator and character' (268). Royle is speaking of *Mrs Dalloway* here, of its thematic and structural concerns with telepathy, and of his own very understandable preference for a notion of narrative telepathy over the 'religious, panoptical delusion of omniscience' (261). It is partly the very idea of a narrator or a character as a person that is at issue here, and so the possibility of any inference of secret and undisclosed knowledge that might lie behind the words as they present themselves in a novel. In the absence of a mind, it seems pointless to speculate about what a novel might know at some level behind the surface of fictional character, and yet at the same time, there seems to be a knowledge of sorts, a secret, which is the property of neither character nor narrator.

If one account of this secret knowledge is what Perowne doesn't know, either about his own fictionality, the presence of a narrator, and the polemic function that this condition fulfils in the debate on knowledge, there are also other factors to be added to the list, and which might, in a different way be thought of as the secret of literature. Royle's use of *Mrs Dalloway* to analyse the elementary structural relation between character and narrator identifies one common feature between *Saturday* and *Mrs Dalloway*, but to the knowing, the two novels are more profoundly linked than that. Like *Mrs Dalloway*, *Saturday* is set on a single say in London, and involves a symbolic journey across town, and from this point of view, McEwan's novel can also be linked to Joyce's *Ulysses*, and its account of a single day in Dublin. There is a certain thematic baggage that comes with this relation, and with the interest in the single day as a principle of unity, or as a significant unit of time. *Ulysses*, for example, is concerned with the circularity of the day, with the fact that it starts where it finishes, and therefore that it reproduces the circular structure of the 'homecoming' which it parallels in Homer's *Odyssey*. With this parallel also comes an ironic contrast between the temporal limits of the single day, and the epic sweep of the journey of Telemachus and Odysseus, as well as a set of themes of reconciliation between father and son, high and low culture, and between literary and non-literary sensibilities. Both *Mrs Dalloway* and *Ulysses* are concerned at a thematic and technical level with the opposition between internal and external time, and with the enormous quantity of mind activity that fills the smallest units of time. These issues are at work in *Saturday* in a number of ways, in the circularity of its structure, its homecoming themes, its opposition of literature and science, the reconciliation of Perowne with his daughter, and its interest in the encounter of the high-bourgeois world of Perowne with the ordinary criminal culture represented by Baxter. There is in this sense a considerable quantity of significance which is not known either to its main character or to its narrator, and like the structural relation between narrator or character, locates knowledge at a level not represented by any fictional mind or within the scope of omniscience. One important dimension of this knowledge is what the novel knows about time, about the treatment of time in its precursor novels, and about the contemporary conditions in which this tension between subjective and objective time is lived. In his analysis of *Mrs Dalloway* Ricoeur argues that, despite the constant striking of Big Ben throughout the novel, the notion of clock time is inadequate to describe the complex apparatus of public history, collective experience and authority that constitutes the backdrop against which the private thoughts and actions of characters are staged. Borrowing from Nietzsche's phrase 'monumental history' Ricoeur refers to this apparatus as 'monumental time' and describes the special power of novels to know the relation of personal to monumental time in this way:

> We must not stop with a simplistic opposition between clock time and internal time, therefore, but must consider the variety of relations between the concrete temporal experience of various characters and monumental time. The variations on the theme of this relation lead fiction well beyond the abstract opposition we have just referred to and make of it, for the reader, a powerful means of detecting the infinitely varied way of combining the perspectives of time that speculation by itself fails to mediate. (1985: 108)

Here again we encounter the notion from which the discussion of fictional knowledge started, that a novel is capable of more than abstract speculation, and particularly with regard to this infinite variation of relations between the concrete temporal experiences of various characters and monumental time.

Perowne's variation on this theme begins, like Astrid's, before dawn in the vision of what seems at first to be a meteor crossing the London sky, and which turns out to be a burning plane heading for Heathrow. Like *Mrs Dalloway*, this is a novel which shows a constant interest in the linearity of clock time, and through constant reference to clocks, the reader always knows the time to within a few minutes. The importance of this incident at the beginning of Perowne's day is partly the role it performs in transforming clock time into monumental time, since it is through the rolling reports of TV news that this incident passes from the realm of a private occurrence into the public domain. The news is a kind of clock for Perowne, by which he measures his private experiences,[5] but it is also the unfolding story of the historical day, through which the contemporary historical context of the day, and most particularly the mass protest against the war in Iraq which took place on that day, find their way into the novel. Perowne's chance vision of the burning plane, like his interaction with the anti-war demonstration as he attempts to go about his day in London, situates his individual life in relation to historical events in the traditional manner of the historical novel, but the relation between the rolling time of Perowne's thought and the rolling events of TV and radio news constitutes the novel's dynamic of temporal experience and monumental time. Like Astrid's interest in digital video, one of the functions of this tension is the enactment of a distinctly modern relation between the present and its representation as retrospect, a relation which seems to define the reality of an event in terms of its representation:

> It's time for the news. Once again the radio pulses, the synthesised bleeps, the sleepless anchor and his dependable jaw. And there it is, made real at last, the plane askew on the runway, apparently intact, surrounded by firefighters still spraying foam, soldiers, police, flashing lights, and ambulances backed up and ready. Before the story, irrelevant praise for the rapid response of the emergency services. Only then is it explained. (2005: 35)

The retrospect of news is a form of explanation of the kind that Perowne values over the reinventions of literature, a mastery which is lacking in the experiential present, and which bestows on the event the authority of the real. The relation here between Perowne's subjectivity and monumental time is notably different from that of Clarissa Dalloway, partly as a result of the sense of corroboration between the public narratives of news and private experience. This sense of the gap between public and private, on which the interaction between Astrid and Amber is structured, extends more generally to Perowne's relation to his historical moment, and to his position in the modern city, which is one of 'aggressive celebration of the times' (78). His historical self-consciousness is characterised chiefly as a feeling of comfort, in which his scientific turn of mind is at home in the age of wondrous machines:

> Dense traffic is heading into the city for Saturday night pleasures just as the first wave of coaches is bringing the marchers out. During the long crawl towards the lights at Gypsy Corner, he lowers his window to taste the scene in full – the bovine patience of a jam, the abrasive tang of icy fumes, the thunderous idling machinery in six lanes east and west, the yellow street light bleaching colour from the bodywork, the jaunty thud of entertainment systems, the red tail lights stretching away ahead into the city, white headlights pouring out of it. He tries to see it, or feel it, in historical terms, this moment in the last decades of the petroleum age, when a nineteenth-century device is brought to final perfection in the early years of the twenty-first; when the unprecedented wealth of masses at serious play in the unforgiving modern city makes for a sight that no previous age can have imagined. Ordinary people! Rivers of light. He wants to make himself see it as Newton might, or his contemporaries, Boyle, Hooke, Wren, Willis – those clever men of the English Enlightenment who for a few years held in their minds nearly all the world's science. Surely they would be awed. Mentally he shows it off to them: this is what we've done, this is commonplace in our time. (167–8)

In this passage the entire chain of association is visible between the technological conditions of the modern city and Perowne's place in it, as he envisages a past of which he is the culmination, and a future in which the petroleum age is over, showing modernity off to the scientists of the past, or light to the Enlightenment. His position of mastery over the present, his spokesmanship for and inclusion in it, attest to a general commensurability between his inner life and the public world which is also reflected in his very attitude to time. He is committed to linearity, to the idea of progress, to clock time, and to the public narratives which are attached to clock time in the form of news. If *Mrs Dalloway* offers a variant of the relation of internal to monumental time in which the anachronicity of the former confronts the relentless forward motion of the latter, *Saturday* corroborates the scientific mind style with its monumental history. In this respect he contrasts with his mother, whose Alzheimer's delivers everything into the present, and whose relation to time is less than rational: 'I put sap in the clock' she's telling him 'to make it moist' (166). This association of temporal disorder with insanity is, for Perowne, part of a general structure of oppositions between insanity and sanity, which places the 'bad dream' of his mother's illness with the dream-like qualities of the supernatural and the experiments with time that he abhors in the contemporary novel as the other to his own sanity:

> Dreams don't interest him; that this should be real is a richer possibility. And he's entirely himself, he is certain of it, and he knows that sleep is behind him: to know the difference between it and waking, to know the boundaries, is the essence of sanity. (4)

As Perowne wakes up, like Gregor Samsa, into his nightmare the denunciation of dreams, like his denunciation of literature at the start of the novel, operates in conjunction with its own denial, as the structural dependence of his sanity upon what he does not know. As Perowne's day is surrounded by night, so too is his waking sanity surrounded by the insanity of dreams, and the unknowable conditions in which his fictional life is embedded, and these conditions must include what he doesn't know of his own intertextual relations to *The Odyssey*, *Ulysses* and *Mrs Dalloway*.

The Accidental and *Saturday* are both set in 2003 and published in 2005, they both seem to link a certain preoccupation of time with the spirit of the times, and they both deal with the intrusion into the life of a family of an outsider. But in one important respect I have argued that they are fundamentally different, since I claimed that *The Accidental* knows what it knows about time, and now I am claiming that *Saturday* knows what it knows only unconsciously, through a conjunction between what is known and what is unknown or unknowable. Because *Saturday* is vigilant in the preservation of its realistic frame, its self-knowledge is necessarily incomplete, since it cannot show even the most basic awareness of its own fictionality, and so of its own place in the debate between literature and science. *Saturday* differs from *The Accidental* in the sense that the former maintains an entirely implicit self-knowledge in its dramatisation of reflections upon literature, where the latter develops its self-knowledge in an explicit way, principally through its anti-realistic frame-breaking. Is it really possible to uphold this distinction, between implicit and explicit self-knowledge? On what grounds might one distinguish between conscious self-consciousness and unconscious self-consciousness, or between a novel that knows what it knows and one that doesn't? It is quite clear that the question of knowledge and the appeal to consciousness, and by extension to unconsciousness, and by further extension to conscious and unconscious self-consciousness bring with them a theory of mind which would view fictional writing as externality to some inner depth, just as de Bolla's Newman painting might be the external manifestation of knowledge which it refuses to yield, and so must remain secret knowledge. It is also clear that in retreat from a model of conscious knowledge which is too straightforward, both Miller and Royle have resorted to Derrida's concept of the secret, and the essential relationship between literature and the secret. A close examination of the relations between surface and depth in this passage is required to see how it might differ from the first theory of mind. The passage in question is as follows:

> Here we touch on the structure of a secret about which literary fiction tells us the essential, or which tells us, in return, the essential concerning the possibility of a literary fiction. If the secret remains undetectable, unbreakable, in this case, if we have no chance of ever knowing whether counterfeit money was actually given to the beggar, it is first of all because there is no sense in wondering what actually happened, what was the true intention of the narrator's friend and the meaning hidden 'behind' his utterances. No more incidentally than behind the utterances of the narrator. As these fictional characters have no consistency, no depth beyond their literary phenomenon, the absolute inviolability of the secret they carry depends first of all on the essential superficiality of their phenomenality, on the *too-obvious* of that which they present to view. (Derrida 1992b: 153)

The secret being referred to here is a straightforward example. In Baudelaire's tale 'Counterfeit Money', the narrator and his friend have given a beggar some money, but the narrator's friend has given considerably more, an act of generosity which he justifies with the words 'It was the counterfeit coin'. The secret that Derrida is discussing here is the answer to the question of whether the justification is true. In this eternal enigma, then, which refuses itself 'to any promise of deciphering or hermeneutic', Derrida finds an essential secret which fiction tells us about, and which in turn tells us about the essential nature of fiction. The second of these claims is presumably very modest: that in fiction, there are cases in which the truth of the situation can never be known, and because fiction is not real, because its characters have no depth beyond the words on the page, there is no possible investigation of the enigma. This second claim remains open to the possibility that in life, the investigation of enigmas might offer more hope, of some discovery of the facts behind surfaces, and that real people have depth that fictional characters lack. The first claim, however, is considerably more significant in scope: that this condition is in fact a general one, which fiction tells us about, explicitly that the essential superficiality of fictional characters and the absolute indecipherability of their enigmas might offer a model for all such enigmas outside of fiction, as well as the enigma of fiction itself. Before we let this passage speak again, we can extend the significance of this secret from one which is internal in a particular fiction (what a character does or does not know) to the idea of fictional knowledge (what a novel does or does not know) and argue by extension that it is pointless to wonder what a novel actually knows, since a novel has no depth beyond its literary phenomenon. The next three sentences of this passage are as follows:

> This inviolability depends on nothing other than the altogether bare device of being-two-to-speak [l'être-deux-à-parler] and it is the possibility of non-truth in which every possibility of truth is held or is made. It thus says the (non-) truth of literature, let us say the secret *of* literature: what literary fiction tells us about the secret, of the (non-) truth of the secret, but also a secret whose possibility assures the possibility of literature. Of the secret kept both as thing or as being, as thing thought, and as technique. (1992b: 153)

The ambiguity of whether we are talking about a secret which is internal to a particular literary text or which is an essential characteristic of literature, whether the secret belongs to literature or pertains to literature, is encapsulated here by Derrida's double genitive: the secret *of* literature (his italics). In this case, the ambiguity is between a very ordinary point, that we cannot know truth in literature, and an excessively profound one, that the secret is the essential characteristic of literature. Each detail in the argument, then resonates suggestively between the banal and the portentous. The 'being-two-to-speak' can be both the conversation in Baudelaire's tale and the essential relation to the other which is the foundational possibility of language in general, while 'the (non-) truth of literature' can be both the internal feature of the counterfeit coin or the essential structural relation of literature to truth. It is the ambiguity of the secret conceived as the object of knowledge (the thing thought) and technique (the way in which it is thought). This constant slippage between the internal details of the literary work and the essential conditions of literature is what gives Derrida's discussions of literary texts their essentially thematic atmosphere, giving the impression that theoretical issues are conducted at the level of thematic content in the text, and that their topics are allegories for their own techniques. It is also what allows the most grandiose claims about the nature of literature and language to take refuge in the alibi of their local and limited significance. The other significant problem with the argument of this passage is that it seems to want to preserve and abolish the model of surface and depth which underlies the idea of knowledge, or of the idea of language as pure externality. On one hand, there is a claim that, because we can never enquire behind the surfaces of fictional characters, the secret of literature, which literature tells us about, is that it is pointless to try. On the other hand, the absolute inviolability of the secret results from this superficiality. The first claim offers a model of pure surface, pure externality, beyond which it is pointless to enquire, but the persistence of the secret, the very existence of a secret depends on the notion that there is something to enquire into, or something which lies behind the surface. If we suppose that this is the situation that Derrida wishes to describe, one which both abolishes and preserves the model of surface and depth, the model of reading on offer would be one in which we make inferences about the inner lives of fictional characters based on the assumption of depth behind the phenomenal surface, and at the same time know that it is inviolable: we would enquire into a secret and know that there isn't one. This is a perfectly reasonable situation, particularly since we might be bringing a theory of mind to the reading of a literary text which is not normally for use in relation to a fictional world, but one fashioned in the outside world, in which the inquiry into secrets, into depths behind surfaces, is not impeded by the essential superficiality of fictional characters. How then are we to understand the relation between surface and depth in fiction and the relation between surface and depth outside of fiction, or between an internal secret in a literary text and the light that this kind of internal secret might shed on secrets more generally? The answer to this lies in the word 'possibility'. Again this is an argumentative manoeuvre that Derrida repeats throughout his writing, and which we have already encountered in the definition of the logic of supplementarity, as the possibility which produces that to which it is said to be added on. The relation between the secret in Baudelaire's tale and a theory of mind that would apply outside of that tale is not one of simple generalisation. The claim is not that all language, like the sentence which may or may not lie about the counterfeit coin, is pure externality. It is that the possibility established in the fictional domain, the possibility of surface without depth, is a possibility that the other model, of surface as the externality of depth, cannot get away from: 'the possibility of non-truth in which every possibility of truth is held or is made'.

If, when it comes to the internal consciousness of time, the novel picks up where the philosophy of time leaves off, it might best be thought of in these terms. We have explored several kinds of knowledge which the novel might have about time, but in each case it is knowledge which hides behind the surface of fiction, in the sense that it is not explicitly stated. There is the open discussion of time engaged in by a character or narrator, the representation of inner time-consciousness, the symbolic episode as an inquiry into time, allusion and reference to other novels about time, the relationship between fictional time and narrative time, and the relationship between fictional time and the material textuality of the book. The first of these, the open reflection on time engaged in by a narrator or character, is probably the only one that is in any way explicit, but it is also the most trivial and least novelistic. Of course, this explicit reflection might also entail discussion of the novel form itself, or of the nature of memory, recording and writing, but even so this would be the kind of knowledge that we might find in philosophy, narratology, criticism and theory, and tells us nothing of the kind of knowledge that the novel can develop after these discourses have left off. We only have to put explicit reflection on time into a relationship with the temporality of fiction, as *The Accidental* does, to produce a more complicated inquiry into time, one which is no longer on the surface of language but exists in a relationship or a tension between what a novel says and what it does. Fiction, in this sense, always has a secret about time, a knowledge which necessarily lies beneath the surface, and yet which also refuses the very idea of surface and depth which the notion of fictional knowledge offers. If a fictional character is essentially superficial, and any secret is therefore absolutely inviolable, so too must fictional knowledge of time be regarded as pure phenomenality, without depth beyond its literary phenomenon, and its secret knowledge about time as absolutely inviolable. But the possibility of this surface without depth is not a reason to discard the notion of depth, or the model of knowledge altogether, since it is the possibility of the inviolable secret from which philosophy and narrative theory have to begin. The novel may take up where philosophy leaves off, but the possibility of doing so seems inaugural for the discourse it carries on from, like a future possibility which produces the moment to which it is said to be added on.

Notes

1. I owe this recognition of the literal meaning of 'literal' to Derek Attridge and his work on Joyce's non-lexical onomatopoeia in *Ulysses*. (Joyce's Noises', paper delivered at The London Modernism Seminar, 12 November 2005.)
2. 'This is a quintessential place. Her mother keeps saying so, she says it every evening' (Smith 2005: 11).
3. 'The sun has come out on most of the dawns she has recorded. This is what a good summer is like. In the past, before she was born, the summers were better, they were perpetual beautiful summers from May to October in the past apparently' (11); 'The sun has been hitting that stone every summer all that time, right the way through the perpetual summers up to the ecologically worrying ones of now' (127).
4. See Eco 1994.
5. 'It's five days since they made love, Monday morning, before the six o'clock news, during a rainstorm . . .' (McEwan 2005: 23).

Chapter 8

Tense Times

The argument about the relationship between time and narrative is now coming into focus. It begins in the Kantian notion that we have no access to things in themselves, but only, as phenomenology holds, to things as they are experienced, apprehended in consciousness, thought about, or understood. But the concept of consciousness cannot be taken for granted. Philosophy in general, both in the phenomenological and in the Anglo-American analytical traditions, has turned to language in order to investigate the realms of experience, perception, thought and understanding. If consciousness is fundamentally linguistic, it follows that we ought to be able to study what we think of as phenomena, or the only reality to which we have access, through linguistic forms. There are philosophers and linguists who have taken this approach to the relationship between linguistic forms and metaphysics: that some understanding of reality can be reached through the analysis of linguistic forms, and even that some understanding of what time is can be reached through an analysis of temporal reference in language, and particularly through the understanding of tense. What has not really been done is to apply this argument specifically to narrative, and therefore to move not only between linguistics and metaphysics, but to infer from the tense structure of narrative a metaphysics of time.

We have, in the terminology supplied to us by Genette, a basic framework for the description of tense in narrative, but there is much more work to be done on the relevance of tense in narratology, and particularly so because the study of tense in relation to linguistic and logical structure has been a fertile area of philosophy over the last few decades. Here we find ourselves switching between what are often, and misleadingly,[1] called the Continental and Anglo-American traditions of philosophy. While many of the perspectives explored so far in this study have their roots in the structuralist and phenomenological traditions of European thought, the major contributions to an understanding of tense have evolved in British and American philosophy. It is one of the aims of this concluding chapter to bring these discourses into conversation, but it is also reasonable to claim that this is one of the areas in which these apparently separate traditions of philosophy have encountered and used each other's insights. It might also not be too much of an exaggeration to assert that this is also the domain in which the philosophy of time comes into closest contact with the approaches to time in the physical sciences. It is therefore the aim of this chapter to identify and analyse the ways in which the study of narrative can learn from the philosophy of tense, and the ways in which this relationship between narrative and tense map onto the debates surrounding time in the physical sciences. As before, the direction of teaching is not one-directional, from philosophy to literature. It will also be suggested here that an understanding of the temporal structure of fictional narrative, and of narrative in general, offers a kind of access, perhaps the only access we have, to what might be called the 'reality' of time.

The relationship between narrative time and tense can be approached through the slightly, but only slightly, less complex question of the tense structure of the English verb. David Crystal argues that we are all misled into a simplified understanding of tense by the schoolroom notion that there are fundamentally three tenses which correspond to the three logical time zones of past, present and future, a conception of tense which derives from the ending-based tense structure of Latin. Crystal has some fun with this idea, demonstrating that the present tense alone can be used to refer to the present, the past and the future in an indefinite number of permutations. The form of the present tense in the English verb, in other words, does not guarantee that the time reference will be to the present. Hence, the newspaper headline which declares 'Jim Smith Dies' uses the present to refer to the past, and the utterance 'I hear you've found a new flat' refers to an act of hearing which may have happened some time ago. This recognition about tense, Crystal argues, is one of the major contributions of linguistic accounts of English grammar in the past century, namely that there is 'no straightforward correlation between the use of a present-tense form and the reference to present time', that 'one linguistic form can have several time references' and that 'one time reference can be expressed by several different forms' (Crystal 2002: 112). This might be thought a bad sign for the analytical purchase of tense on time reference, but it is easy to jump to the wrong conclusion here. The fact that the tense form of the verb does not correspond to a particular time reference is by no means a catastrophe for the analysis of tense. Rather it points to the importance of an understanding of tense which does not place the entire burden of time-reference on the verb. Crystal,

and many other analysts of tense have shown that tense operates at a discursive level higher than the tense-form of the verb, for example through
indexical references such as 'yesterday', 'today' and 'tomorrow'. It is
straightforward, for example, to produce a reference to future time in the
present tense with the use of such an indexical: 'I am leaving for France
tomorrow'. In miniature, this illustrates an important principle for the
relation between tense and time: that time reference cannot be located in
the verb itself, so that the analysis of temporal structure must look to
other features of a sentence, or to larger units of discourse than the verb
form itself. For this reason, for example, a narrative which is written in
the present tense should not be thought of as being tensed (in the philosophical sense) differently from one written in a past tense, since the time
reference to the past is not determined by the tense of its verbs. The
divorce between tense and verb forms is rather like the recognition in
narratology that a so-called first-person narrative voice does not corre-
late to the observation of first-person pronouns. Genette's preference for
the terms 'intradiegetic' and 'extradiegetic' over the traditional categories of first-person and third-person voice is a recognition of a fallacy
which is similar in nature to that of the correlation of verb-tense with
temporal reference: the fallacy that there is a formal linguistic basis on
which these aspects of narratological description are founded. There is
some reason for retaining the terminology of tense in relation to temporal reference in narrative, but the understanding of tense on which the
terminology is based must come from philosophy rather than grammar.
It is a commonplace of the philosophy of time in the analytical tradition
that philosophical positions on time fall into two basic camps which are
known as the *tensed* and the *untensed* or *tenseless* views of time respectively. These two views, and their relationship to narrative, require
further exposition, but for the moment serve as a justification for the
retention of the terminology of tense in this discussion, despite the chasm
between the linguistic verb form and its temporal reference.

Crystal's demonstration of the complexity of the relationship between
temporal reference and verb tense has some very interesting implications
for the idea that it might be possible to move inferentially from linguistic structure to metaphysical propositions about time. But this is not the
direction that Crystal's own inquiry takes in the analysis presented in
'Talking About Time'. The demonstration of the complexity of temporal
reference in this analysis is followed by a discussion of what he calls the
'literary dimension' of talking about time. Far from inferring anything
about the nature of time from the temporal structure of language, this
section reverts to a kind of content-based citation of literature in which
time is addressed explicitly as a topic. We are offered Dylan Thomas

reflecting on the nature of time in *Under Milk Wood* and T. S. Eliot's invocation of Aboriginal time in *Burnt Norton*. Perhaps more astonishing in its failure to take on board the implications of his own argument is the citation of a passage from *As You Like It*, in which Rosalind explains to Orlando the 'diverse paces with divers persons' with which time passes, and from which discussion he draws the following staggering conclusion: 'This early instance of temporal relativity, anticipating Einsteinian insights by some 300 years, brings us closer to the way in which some cultures routinely think of time, as a relative, dynamic, influential, living force, and express it in their verb forms, vocabulary, idiom, and figurative expression' (2002: 123). There is, in this transfer of attention from the structures of tense in a language to the explicit thematisation of time in literature a reflection of what we might call the problem of time in literary criticism, that is, the retreat from formal and linguistic aspects of temporal structure to mere citations and paraphrases of literary statements about time. If literature really says something about time in the sense that it makes some contribution to metaphysical reflections on time, it will be analysed by a serious effort to understand the temporal structure of its discourses rather than by the citation and paraphrase of its statements by a content-based criticism. In Crystal's article this is all the more surprising because the consideration of literature follows from a brief discussion of the linguistic-anthropological approach to the question of time. According to the anthropological view, commonly associated with Benjamin Lee Whorf, our sense of reality is directly associated with the structure of language, and therefore, when it comes to time, the 'metaphysics of time' which operates in a culture can be accessed by analysing the structures of language of that culture. One of the obvious consequences of this view is that any analysis that upholds it will be indifferent to the explicit content of a discourse and therefore any open statements about time that it may make. Instead it will aim to identify the metaphysical suppositions about time which are inherent in the system and structure of a particular language. Crystal, following Whorf, offers a range of observations which work from linguistic structures to a concept of time: the Hopi tense system and its lack of past and future tenses; the attachment of tensed endings to words that are not verbs in Potawatomi and Japanese; and the use of the same word to signify 'yesterday' and 'tomorrow' in Arrernte and Wik-Mungkan to name three. These examples seem to suggest that some kind of concept of time can be read off from aspects of a language system, that is from the 'formal ways in which languages express time relationships' (2002: 116). Why then, when Crystal turns to literature, does he retreat from the view that a concept of time can be discerned in the formal ways in which literature expresses time relationships to one in which time is addressed at the level of theme and content? When looking for a tense-based perspective on the metaphysics of time in narrative, the argument that time-reference is not directly correlated to verb tense offers an interesting premise, while the practice of discovering passages which thematise time in literature offers something disappointingly pre-critical.

A-Series and B-Series Semantics

The real possibilities for a narratology informed by tense philosophy are indicated by, among other works, Peter Ludlow's thesis in *Semantics, Tense and Time*, the basic goal of which is to 'illustrate how one can study metaphysical questions from a linguistic/semantical perspective'. Interestingly, Ludlow also begins from Whorf's anthropology, and the claim that the reality of time can be inferred from the structure of language. For Ludlow, however, this is not the same as a claim that some contingent, culturally different concept of time can be inferred from the language of a particular culture, but rather, as he claims, the generative grammar of the past few decades has shown us, that 'the differences between human languages are superficial at best' (Ludlow 1999: xiii):

> I think that on a certain level of deep analysis his [Whorf's] description of the Hopi tense system was basically correct – not just for the Hopi, but for all of us. That is, I think that a close study of English does not support the thesis that there is such a thing as tense – at least not the sort of tense system that is compatible with currently favoured philosophical theories of time. (1999: xiv)

Ludlow is quite sure that speakers of English in fact conform to the claim made of the Hopi, that we have 'no words, grammatical forms, constructions or expressions that refer directly to what we call "time", or to past, present or future.' Like Crystal then he is sceptical in regard to the possibility of reading metaphysical beliefs from verb tenses alone, but confident nevertheless that metaphysical commitments about the reality of time are entailed in the structures of language. In other words 'tense' here means something more than verb tense, and the study of this enlarged notion of tense will therefore offer a 'way of studying metaphysical questions from a linguistic perspective'. By following the argument about tense, therefore, it is possible to develop a theory of narrative tense which is capable of analysing what narratives say about time without resort to the kind of thematic or content-based analysis that we find in Crystal's argument, and which prevails to such a surprising extent in commentaries on the contemporary novel.

The distinction between A-series and B-series theories of time, which has been so entrenched in the philosophy of time in the analytical tradition, is capable of some important contributions to an understanding of narrative, and particularly so when it operates, as Ludlow's argument does, by moving between linguistics and metaphysics. The theory based on an A-series conception of time (A-theory) normally holds that the future and the past do not exist, and that existence therefore is presence. It is possible to say only that the events of the past did exist, and that the events of the future will exist, but these events are *tensed* in relation to the present, to now, which is thought of as having special ontological properties. The A-theory is therefore a tensed theory of time, and goes by a variety of other names such as *presentism* and the *moving now* theory. B-theory, on the other hand, dispenses with the idea of the now, and therefore with the idea of events being past and future. Time, according to B-theory, is a sequence of events all of which are equally real, and between which the only relations are those of *earlier than* and *later than*, and the idea of 'now' or 'the present' is merely psychological. B-theory is therefore *untensed*, and is often thought of as an objective and essentially spatial way of understanding events, as if time were spread out like a landscape. A-theory gives time *properties* (the properties of being present, past or future) while B-theory views time in terms of *relations* (of being earlier or later than). The interesting thing about the B-theory, especially for our purposes, is that though it denies any special ontological status to the present, or indeed any real ontological difference between the past and the future, it is not quite true to say that it dispenses with the ideas of present, past and future altogether. B-theory explains what we mean when we view something to be past, present or future as just that: something that we 'mean' or something which is an effect of linguistic meaning. The idea of the past, for example, is something which comes into being only when some utterance produces it. If I say that my fifteenth birthday is in the past, what I mean, according to B-theorists, is that it is earlier than the event of my saying that it is in the past, and similarly, 'now' and 'in the future' just mean 'the time of this utterance' and 'later than this utterance'. The relation between the present, the past and the future, which is encoded in linguistic tense, is therefore just a way of placing events in relation to the utterances which refer to them, so that A-properties can simply be translated into B-relations. Reciprocally, the A-theorist characteristically views the earlier than/later than relations of the B-series as a scheme which simply asserts the properties of presence, pastness and futurity in a way that seeks to eliminate the subjectivity and the special ontological status on which the idea of presence rests. In the analytical tradition it has generally been assumed that these perspectives are incompatible, and that the philosopher, and indeed the theoretical physicist, is obliged to choose between tensed and untensed conceptions of time.[2] Hence, the fundamental positions on time can be mapped onto these apparently opposing theories from the debate between presentism and eternalism in philosophy to the difference between temporal becoming and the block-view universe in contemporary physics. Clearly Augustine's difficulties surrounding the existence of the present operate according to a tensed account of time, while its opposite, namely the view of eternity as a spatial and static landscape is a perspective available only to God. Those theories of time, both before and after Kant, which hold that the object of study can be only that which is accessible to the human consciousness also hold that there can be no access to the B-series conception of time: that it is an essentially non-human perspective.[3]

How might the A-series/B-series distinction work when it comes to the theory or narrative, and particularly to fictional narrative? I observed in Chapter 1 that the phenomenology of reading a novel differed from the phenomenology of life more generally insofar as the future, in a novel, is not absolutely open. In the written text, the future lies in wait in a specific way, in that it is possible to flout the linearity of writing and take an excursion into the future. I can abandon the *moving now* of fiction, the place of the bookmark, and skip ahead at will. I do not require the wormhole of authorially controlled prolepsis for such an excursion, in the sense that I can leaf through the novel and seize on any moment of the fictional future. In this sense the fictional future is not really open, because events in the future are already written and awaiting my arrival, and this can be verified by actually visiting them out of turn. This is most obvious in the case of a novel that I have read before, where I know for certain what is to come, and have to feign to myself, or reconstruct, the experience of not knowing. It is one of the features of the B-series that it does not give any special ontological privilege to the present, and that it views all moments, including 'future events', to have an equal status. As a temporal structure it might appear as if the fictional narrative represents, artificially, a B-theory of time in the sense that its time sequence is laid out spatially as a book, and that all moments of that sequence exist equally, co-temporaneously as written words. Whereas the existence of the future is controversial in extra-fictional human time, it is much less controversial to claim that the fictional future already exists. The discourses of fatalism and determinism regularly borrow from this feature of writing, whether fictional or not, to describe the future as in some way *written*, or *scripted*, since something that has a script does not have an open future. The privilege of the present is undermined by writing, and so too is the asymmetry between the past and future, since the future is no more open, no more affected by decision and choice than is the past. It would seem then that the world of written narrative (let us stick for the moment with fictional narrative) presents a B-series of a more certain kind than is ever given in 'lived experience'. And yet there is also a kind of experiential present at work in the reading of fiction. When Peter Brooks talks about reading as the decoding of the preterite tense as a kind of present, he refers to a kind of tensed sense that the reader makes of fictional retrospect, living the events through the moving now of the reader's present (Brooks 1984: 22). According to this moving now, reading is like life, to the extent that the events that have been read are like those that have been lived. They become part of the past. They are remembered in their sequence, and as explanations for the situation of the present. The future, on the other hand, has all the semblance of the extra-fictional future. It is open, often unpredictable, and the subject of anticipations, fears and desires. In previous chapters I have claimed that fictional narrative in various ways forges together anticipation and retrospect, as the anticipation of retrospect. Prolepsis, as we have seen, does this by incorporating into the present a future from which that present will be viewed, whether that future is a fictional event or the event of its reading. The double time of detective fiction gives prolepsis an elaborate power to conjoin the forwards motion of narration to the backwards motion of explanation, and therefore to instruct the experience of events in the light of their outcome. In terms of the debate between A-theory and B-theory, a similar claim can be made for fictional narrative: that fictional narrative is characterised by its special power to articulate a tensed theory of time to an untensed theory of time, though it may be that this is no more than the demonstration of how preposterous it was to separate the two in the first place.

This is a rather bold claim, but it is one that can be supported relatively easily by an analysis of the tense conditions of fiction. The phrase 'tense conditions' here has to be distinguished from any straightforward conception of verb tense. As Crystal's argument indicates, the analysis of tense, and therefore the analysis of temporal structure in discourse must be enlarged beyond the notion of verb tense in order to account adequately for the complex system of time reference. Ludlow's argument is similar, insofar as it points to aspects of tense that are not encoded in the verb, and uses these aspects to test semantic theories which advance A-theories and B-theories of time. At the core of the argument is a claim that I would want to distance my own argument from, in ways that will become clear, that the A-series of time corresponds more closely to reality than the B-series. 'Metaphysics' Ludlow believes 'is, in part, the study of what is real' (1999: 1), and by extension, the ability of A-series and

B-series based semantic theories to cope with the complexities of temporal structure in language will tell us important things about which conception of time is more effective, as it were, in the study of reality.
Ludlow's interest lies in indexicals and temporal anaphora, that is those
words which point to times past, present and future which are not part
of the verb form. His aim is therefore double: on one hand he seeks to
show that B-series approaches to time cannot account semantically for
these aspects of language as adequately as A-series semantics, and on the
other hand, to show that weaknesses which have been identified in
A-theory can be defended or even repaired. I am not going to analyse the
account Ludlow offers of A-series semantics and its ability to explain
indexicals and temporal anaphora. I am interested, however, in the
defence he mounts for A-theory in general and the critique he develops
of the B-series account from linguistic premises. In the first place, then,
let us consider the principal problems with the A-series account of time.
The most famous objection is McTaggart's, who originally formulated
the problem by arguing that the A-theory is essential to any coherent
conception of time, but also that it is contradictory, and therefore that
time cannot be real (McTaggart 1908). The argument is as follows. The
A-theory, according to McTaggart is committed to the idea of change,
and as many commentators since McTaggart have pointed out, the
metaphors used to describe this commitment to change are generally
ideas of motion, passing and flowing. Hence, the river characteristically
offers an account of perpetual change through the metaphor of flowing
water, where the water that will flow past one's Wellington boots is still
upstream, the water that is flowing past them is in front of one's eyes,
and the water that did flow past them is now downstream. In this scheme,
the importance of past, present and future is evident. If, for analytical
purposes we decide to name a single molecule of water M, we can say
that in relation to an observer standing in the river, M is in the first place,
when it is upstream of the observer, in the future, then subsequently it is
present and within the eyeshot of the observer, and thereafter is downstream and therefore in the past. Clearly this is not a *moving now* conception of time. The *now*, by this metaphor, is staying still while events
flow or pass. Nevertheless, according to A-theory M has the properties
of being future, past and present at different times, and because these
properties are incompatible – because something cannot be past and
future, or present and future – McTaggart claims that A-theory leads to
contradiction. The standard objection here is that it is, of course, perfectly possible for something to be past, present and future, just not at
the same time. The whole point about the A-theory is that it arranges
time in terms of these properties, but these properties *change*: events

change from being future to being present to being past. M therefore does have the property of being future, the property of being present and the property of being past, but not at the same time. McTaggart considers this to be an inadmissible defence on the grounds that it involves an invocation of the B-theory which holds that time is a sequence in order to separate the incompatible ontological properties advanced by the A-theory. This part of McTaggart's argument can appear quite foolish, but the way in which it is foolish tells us something useful, and particularly so about time and narrative. It is clear that McTaggart's problem lies in viewing the B-series and the A-series as incompatible theories. It is certainly clear that the problems with each theory, as they have been analysed over the last century, lie in those aspects which each theory, taken in isolation, abandon as the property of the other. An adequate theory of time must be both tensed and tenseless: it must be capable of accounting for the properties of past, present and future, and at the same time be capable of analysing the more objective relations of *earlier than* and *later than*. McTaggart's claim that it is somehow cheating for an A-theorist to invoke the B-series is an authoritarian defence of a distinction which should not have been upheld in the first place, when it is the very necessity of a compatibilist combination of A-series and B-series which is the principal insight yielded by the attempt to hold them in opposition. The problem is well known and so is the solution. It is fundamentally the same problem as that of Augustine's contrast between the present and eternity, and phenomenology's opposition between temporality and cosmological time, and its solution normally takes the form of a recognition that presentism isn't intelligible without borrowing some of the conceptual resources of its other – the idea of sequence or objective time – while the idea of sequence lacks any ability to account for time in the way that it is lived and perceived by human beings.

Before we return to the relevance of tense in the analysis of narrative, and the question of what narrative tells us about the tensed and tenseless theories of time, it is worth analysing the link between the A/B distinction and the Augustinian aporias of time. Augustine's key analogy between time and the recitation of a psalm is particularly suggestive for narratology:

> Suppose that I am going to recite a psalm that I know. Before I begin my faculty of expectation is engaged by the whole of it. But once I have begun, as much of the psalm as I have removed from the province of expectation and relegated to the past now engages my memory, and the scope of the action which I am performing is divided between the two faculties of memory and expectation, the one looking back to the part which I have already recited, the other looking forward to the part which I have still to recite. But my faculty of attention is

present all the while and through it passes what was the future in the process of becoming the past. As the process continues, the province of memory is extended in proportion as that of expectation is reduced, until the whole of my expectation is absorbed. This happens when I have finished my recitation and it has all passed into the province of memory. (Augustine 1961: 278)

Like the river, the analogy of the psalm provides a model for the flow of time in relation to a witness: the river's static witness becomes the presence of 'my faculty of attention', through which the words of the psalm pass, transforming the future into memory. It is of course possible to view the relation of motion and stasis differently. Instead of a static witness, through which water or words flow, we might equally posit a static landscape through which a witness journeys, or a static structure of words through which the reader or recital makes active progress. The advantage of the analogy of the psalm is that, as a scripted discourse, with a verbal structure determined in advance, there is a clear B-series which allows one to claim that each moment, each part, past, present or future of that discourse does have existence. That is to say, there is some imagined vantage point from which the discourse can be seen as a whole, not as a series of nows strung out in time, but as a structural unity in which all parts have an equivalent ontological status. On the other hand there is also an A-series, which is the now of the reader, in the sense of the bit of the discourse currently under the light of what Augustine calls the faculty of attention. There is a tenseless view of the psalm, which ignores the moving now of the recitation, and postulates a B-series in which different parts relate only through the relations of earlier and later; and there is a tensed view, according to which the only bits of the discourse which exist are the bits currently passing through the faculty of attention, while the remainder wallows in the ontologically secondary realms of expectation and memory. Reading, then, offers a particularly useful model for the interaction of A-theory and B-theory, being an analogy for the pre-scripted landscape and the movement of a subjective witness across it.

The psalm may or may not be a narrative, but even if it is not, the 'forward' motion of reading enables it to function as a model of time, and an illustration of A-theory and B-theory. When the discourse in question is a narrative, the effectiveness of the model is doubled, in the sense that we are not only waiting for, or reaching towards, words from the future, but words which are the carriers of events. For a written narrative, the existence of the future is material, in the form of graphic signs or pages ahead, and it is referential. McTaggart's argument can now be restated in a way that is more obviously related to fictional narrative. He claims, in *The Unreality of Time*, that in order for things to exist in time, events must be ordered in relation to a B-series and an A-series: that these two aspects of time must combine to offer an adequate account, but that the two perspectives are in fact incompatible, and therefore that they lead to contradiction. The link between this argument and the question of fictional time is made by McTaggart himself in *The Nature of Existence*, when he considers a possible objection to his argument that time sequences must be thought of in terms of A- and B-series. The objection that McTaggart fends off here is that fictional narrative possesses B-series relations but not A-series properties of time. According to this view, it is not possible to say, of fictional events, that they are past, present or future, but only that one event occurs before or after another. McTaggart claims that, in order for things to be thought of in time at all, they must be thought of in the A-series as well as the B-series, but in the case of fiction, we seem to be faced with events that do occur in time, but which are entirely in the B-series. McTaggart's answer to this objection is that fictional events are not really located in time at all, since they are not existents, but that we nevertheless *imagine* them existing in time, and that to do so entails imagining them in the A-series as well as the B-series. To support this claim, he offers the example of Richard Jeffries' *After London*, a fiction which is set in the future: because we imagine the events of this novel to be located in the future, McTaggart claims, we are imagining fictional events, despite their unreality, to have the property of futurity, and therefore imagining them in the A-series. This is a particularly confusing example, which I would like to contemplate, in order to clarify what it would mean to say that fictional events are imagined in the A-series. If, for example, I think of a novel that is not set in the future, such as Hawthorne's *The Scarlet Letter*, it seems to me critical that I still think of its events as occurring in the future. It may have been written in the 1840s, and set in Puritan Boston, but my attribution of A-series properties to the fictional events is clearly not confined to the location of events in relation to my 'historical now'. The revelation of Hester Prynne's former marriage, and the paternity of her daughter Pearl are future in the sense that they lie in wait of the imagined *now* of reading, whereby the past tense of the narrative is decoded as a kind of present. It may be that the A-properties are complex here, but they are nevertheless A-properties. Hence, I think of Hester's narrative as something that will unfold for me from the future even while it is located, and tensed, in the past in the same way that I might read Jeffries's *After London* and think of it as a future which is located in the past: as what the future used to be like. These two tense structures, of a past which lies ahead, and a future which is past, are inherent in the temporal reference of narrative fiction, and only the surface of a multi-layered conception of 'now' that operates in the reading of fiction.

The reading of a novel, in other words, is tensed, but not only for the reasons given by McTaggart: it is tensed not only in relation to the reader's historical now, but also the now into which the reader is inter-pellated by the fiction, irrespective of history. Gregory Currie develops a different kind of objection to McTaggart's remarks about fiction in 'A Literary Philosophy of Time?' (G. Currie 1999) as part of a general con-sideration of the possibilities that literature might have something to tell us about the nature of time. Currie takes issue with McTaggart's basic claim that to imagine the events of fiction as taking place in time, we must imagine them in the A-series:

> Now I say that the general claim – that imagining events in time involves imag-ining them in the A series – is wrong. On my view, the standard mode of imag-inative involvement with fictions is to imagine that this is occurring before, after, or even contemporaneously with that, but not to imagine either this or that as occurring now, or in the past, or in the future. (1999: 54)

In other words, there is a conception of events in time entailed in the imaginative involvement with ficiton but it is strictly a B-series concep-tion, and therefore McTaggart's claim – that there is no conception of time without the A-series – cannot be right. Let us follow Currie's argu-ment that imaginative involvement with fiction does not involve the A-series. In the first place, he is clear that in order to show that McTaggart is wrong, he is not required to demonstrate that an A-series conception of time is never at work, but only that it is possible to have 'temporally adequate' imaginative involvement which is not tensed. To illustrate this, he turns from fiction to film. The crucial stage of this argu-ment is the next one: 'If we suppose that imaginative involvement with the film requires us to think of its events as tensed, then it seems over-whelmingly plausible that we are to think of them as present' (1999: 55). Watching a film, according to this argument, involves imagining *seeing* the events represented by the film from the point of view of the camera, and therefore imagining seeing them occuring *now*. This is an argument which, as Currie admits, has enjoyed less than universal assent,[4] because of the conflation of the idea of tense with the idea of presence in so-called 'fictional involvement'. The usefulness of film for Currie is that it illus-trates a contradiction in the idea of presence, since films invite a viewer to imagine themselves as a witness within the spatiotemporal world of the film from the point of view of the character, and at the same time (most obviously in cases where fictional characters are alone) as a witness located outside that spatiotemporal world. The contradiction here leads Currie to suppose that imaginative involvement is impersonal, meaning that the events of the fiction are spatiotemporally related to one another but not to us, and therefore that we do not imagine the events of film, or fiction, as past, present or future.

The most striking aspect of this argument for those whose philosophy of time is less rooted in the Anglo-American analytical tradition, is its cavalier use of spatiotemporal presence as a foundational concept. The key step in the argument is the one which links tense to the concept of presence, and it is the logic of this connection which must be questioned. The general argument of this study has returned repeatedly to the proposition that presence requires a kind of self-distance, and particularly that the present is predominantly apprehended as the object of a future memory. Where Gregory Currie argues that A-theory requires that fictional events are imagined as spatiotemporally present, I would suggest instead that a tensed view of fiction cannot operate with a notion of undivided presence as its guiding concept. The role of seeing in Currie's argument is particularly revealing, transposing as it does the supposed opacity of the graphic sign of fiction into the supposed luminosity of film. In fiction we do not see events, and therefore they are not present in the way that Currie intends. Moreover, to have a tensed view of events, we are 'to think of them as present', and yet in the majority of cases the verb structure of narrative fiction invites us to think of them as in the past. There are, as Derrida has reminded us, obvious ways in which the referents – the events of fiction, for example – are absent in writing.

The importance of tense to narratology is that it offers a framework for the analysis of temporal structure and temporal reference in narrative which will go beyond the idea of time as thematic content. This will in turn offer to narratology an exit route from some of the difficulties inherent in the notion of 'about', from which the discussion in this book began, and in particular from Ricoeur's restricting notion that though time is a universal feature of narrative, it is the topic of only of few. The starting point for a tense-based theory of narrative, as I suggested above, might be based in fictional narrative, but would have scope to describe what I have referred to variously as narrative consciousness and narrative as a mode of being. It would begin in fictional narrative for several reasons, perhaps the most important of which is the freedom that fiction possesses to roam in time, and therefore to produce temporal structures of a complicated kind. One aspect of fiction's complicated temporal structure is the special way in which a novel, for example, might possess both A-series properties and B-series relations, even if, as McTaggart claims, the B-series relations of fiction are only of an imaginative kind. A narrative theory which begins in this compatibilism of tensed and untensed accounts of time acquires an ability to explain the proleptic mode of being, the experience of the present as the object of a future memory, which is by no means confined to fiction, and this ability derives partly from the relationship between fiction and life, or what Ricoeur calls the circle of configuration and refiguration. The value of tense-based narratology would therefore extend beyond the description of narrative fiction, and of its increasingly complex temporal structures, to an analysis of the relationship between time and narrative in general. The ability of narrative to produce or transform the human experience of time would be at issue in this analysis, and in a narratology that takes as its starting point the possibility of inferring a metaphysics of time from the temporal structures of narrative.

Notes

1. See Simon Critchley's mini-dissertation on this subject in *Continental Philosophy: A Very Short Introduction.*
2. See for example the scheme proposed by Gale (1968) in which the first characteristic of the A-series is its conviction that the B-series is reducible to the A-series, while the first characteristic of the B-series is vice versa.
3. A comic fictional treatment of the difference between A-theory and B-theory can be found in Kurt Vonnegut's *Slaughterhouse Five.* Here the non-human (Tralfamadorian) conception of time is juxtaposed to the human conception which lives in the moving present. Because the Tralfamadorians see every moment at the same time, there is neither fear of, or regret towards, death, and therefore a moral indifference to the atrocities of the Second World War. The Tralfamadorian block view of the universe also has interesting consequences for the Tralfamarorian novel, which loses all its structural principles, since it is no longer experienced as a temporal sequence (Vonnegut 1991).
4. Currie mentions Levinson (1993) and Lopes (1998), which formulate objections to the longer version of this argument in Gregory Currie (1995).

Bibliography

Amis, Martin (2003) *London Fields*, London: Vintage.

Amis, Martin (2003) *Time's Arrow or The Nature of the Offence*, London: Vintage. First published by Jonathan Cape (1999).

Augustine (1961) *Confessions*, Harmondsworth: Penguin Books.

Barthes, Roland (1968) 'L'effet de réel', *Communications* 11, 84–9.

Booth, Wayne (1961) *The Rhetoric of Fiction*, Chicago: University of Chicago Press.

Borges, Jorge Luis (1964) *Other Inquisitions*, trans. Ruth L. C. Simms, Austin: University of Texas Press.

Brooks, Peter (1984) *Reading for the Plot: Design and Intention in Narrative*, Cambridge, MA, and London: Harvard University Press.

Butterfield, Jeremy (ed.) (1999) *The Arguments of Time*, Oxford: Oxford University Press.

Critchley, Simon (2001) *Continental Philosophy: A Very Short Introduction*, Oxford: Oxford University Press.

Crystal, David (2002) 'Talking About Time', in Ridderbos, K. (ed.), *Time*, Cambridge: Cambridge University Press.

Culler, Jonathan (1983) *On Deconstruction: Theory and Criticism after Structuralism*, London and New York: Routledge.

Culler, Jonathan (1997) *Literary Theory: A Very Short Introduction*, Oxford: Oxford University Press.

Currie, Gregory (1990) *The Nature of Fiction*, Cambridge: Cambridge University Press.

Currie, Gregory (1995) *Image and Mind: Film, Philosophy and Cognitive Science*, Cambridge: Cambridge University Press.

Currie, Gregory (1999) 'Can There Be a Literary Philosophy of Time', in Butterfield, Jeremy (ed.), *The Arguments of Time*, Oxford: Oxford University Press.

Currie, Mark (1998) *Postmodern Narrative Theory*, London: Palgrave/Macmillan.

Dainton, Barry (2001) *Time and Space*, Chesham, Bucks: Acumen.

Danielewski, Mark Z. (2000) *House of Leaves*, London and New York: Doubleday.

Davis, Paul (1995) *About Time: Einstein's Unfinished Revolution*, Harmondsworth: Penguin.

de Bolla, Peter (2001) *Art Matters*, Cambridge, MA: Harvard University Press.

de Man, Paul (1979) *Allegories of Reading: Figural Language in Rousseau,*

Nietzsche, Rilke, and Proust, New Haven, CT, and London: Yale University Press.

Deleuze, Gilles (1994) *Difference and Repetition*, trans. P. Paton, London: Athlone Press.

Derrida, Jacques (1973) *Speech and Phenomena and Other Essays on Husserl's Theory of Signs*, trans. D. Allison, Evanston, IL: Northwestern University Press.

Derrida, Jacques (1974) *Of Grammatology*, trans. Gayatri Spivak, Baltimore, MD, and London: Johns Hopkins University Press.

Derrida, Jacques (1981) *Positions*, trans. A. Bass, London: Athlone.

Derrida, Jacques (1982) *Margins of Philosophy*, trans. Alan Bass, Brighton: The Harvester Press.

Derrida, Jacques (1992a) 'The Law of Genre', in Attridge, D. (ed.), *Acts of Literature*, London and New York: Routledge.

Derrida, Jacques (1992b) *Given Time: I. Counterfeit Money*, trans. Peggy Kamuf, Chicago and London: University of Chicago Press.

Derrida, Jacques (1995) *The Gift of Death*, trans. David Wills, Chicago and London: Chicago University Press.

Derrida, Jacques (1998) *Archive Fever: A Freudian Impression*, trans. Eric Prenowitz, Chicago: Chicago University Press.

Derrida, Jacques (2002) *Without Alibi*, ed. Peggy Kamuf, Stanford, CA: Stanford University Press.

Eco, Umberto (1994) *The Limits of Interpretation*, Bloomington: Indiana University Press.

Eddington, A. S. (1928) *The Nature of the Physical World: Gifford Lectures 1927*, Cambridge: Cambridge University Press.

Gale, Richard (1968) *The Language of Time*, London and New York: Routledge and Kegan Paul.

Genette, Gerard (1980) *Narrative Discourse*, trans. Jane Lewin, Oxford: Basil Blackwell.

Grosz, Elizabeth (2004) *The Nick of Time: Politics, Evolution and the Untimely*, Durham, NH, and London: Duke University Press.

Harvey, David (1989) *The Condition of Postmodernity*, Oxford: Basil Blackwell.

Hawking, Stephen (1995) *A Brief History of Time: From the Big Bang to Black Holes*, London: Bantam Press.

Hawthorne, Nathaniel (1970) *The Scarlet Letter*, Harmondsworth: Penguin Books.

Hegel, G. W. F. (1977) *Phenomenology of Spirit*, trans. A. V. Miller, Oxford: Oxford University Press.

Heidegger, Martin (1962) *Being and Time*, trans. John Macquarrie and Edward Robinson, Oxford: Basil Blackwell.

Heise, Ursula (1997) *Chronoschisms: Time, Narrative and Postmodernism*, Cambridge: Cambridge University Press.

Helm, Bertrand (1985) *Time and Reality in American Philosophy*, Amherst: The University of Massachusetts Press.

Hogg, James (1981) *The Private Memoirs and Confessions of a Justified Sinner*, Oxford and New York: Oxford University Press. First published 1969.

Horwich, Paul (1987) *Asymmetries in Time: Problems in the Philosophy of Science*, London and Cambridge, MA: MIT Press.

Husserl, Edmund (1964) *The Phenomenology of Internal Time-Consciousness*, trans. James Churchill, Bloomington: Indiana University Press.

Husserl, Edmund (1970) *Logical Investigations* (2 vols), trans. J. N. Findlay, London: Routledge and Kegan Paul.

Husserl, Edmund (1999) *The Essential Husserl: Basic Writings in Transcendental Phenomenology*, ed. Donn Welton, Bloomington: Indiana University Press.

Hutcheon, Linda (1988) *A Poetics of Postmodernism: History, Theory, Fiction*, New York and London: Routledge.

Jakobson, Roman (1960) 'Closing Statement', in Sebeok, T. (ed.), *Style in Language*, Cambridge, MA: MIT Press.

Jameson, Fredric (1972) *The Prison House of Language: A Critical Account of Structuralism and Russian Formalism*, Princeton, NJ: Princeton University Press.

Jameson, Fredric (1992) 'Postmodernism and Consumer Society', in Brooker, Peter (ed.), *Modernism/Postmodernism*, London and New York: Longman, pp. 163–79.

Jeffries, Richard (1980) *After London or Wild England*, Oxford: Oxford University Press.

Johnson, Barbara (1980) *The Critical Difference: Essays in the Contemporary Rhetoric of Reading*, Baltimore, MD: Johns Hopkins University Press.

Kant, Immanuel (2003) *Critique of Pure Reason*, trans. Norman Kemp Smith, London and New York: Palgrave.

Kermode, Frank (1966) *The Sense of an Ending: Studies in the Theory of Fiction*, Oxford and New York: Oxford University Press.

Kermode, Frank (1985) *Forms of Attention*, Chicago: University of Chicago Press.

Kierkegaard, Søren (1999) *The Living Thoughts of Kierkegaard* ed. W. H. Anden, New York: New York Review of Books.

Kort, Wesley (1985) *Modern Fiction and Human Time: A Study in Narrative and Belief*, Tampa: University of Florida Presses.

Kuhn, Thomas (1962) *A Theory of Scientific Revolutions*, International Encyclopedia of Unified Science 2:2, Chicago: University of Chicago Press.

Laclau, Ernesto (1996) *Emancipation(s)*, London and New York: Verso.

Levinson, J. (1993) 'Seeing, Imaginarily, at the Movies', *Philosophical Quarterly* 43, 70–8.

Lloyd, Genevieve (1993) *Being in Time: Selves and Narrators in Philosophy and Literature*, London and New York: Routledge.

Lopes, D. M. M. (1998) 'Imagination, Illusion and Experience in Film: Gregory Currie's Image and Mind', *Philosophical Studies* 89, 343–54.

Lucas, J. R. (1984) *Time and Causality: An Essay in Natural Philosophy*, Oxford: Oxford University Press.

Lucas, J. R. (1989) *The Future: An Essay on God, Temporality and Truth*, Oxford: Basil Blackwell.

Ludlow, Peter (1999) *Semantics, Tense and Time: An Essay in the Metaphysics of Natural Language*, Cambridge, MA: MIT Press.

McEwan, Ian (2005) *Saturday*, London: Vintage.

McTaggart, John (1908) 'The Unreality of Time', *Mind*, vol. 17.

McTaggart, John (1927) *The Nature of Existence* (2 vols), Cambridge: Cambridge University Press.

Medina, Angel (1979) *Reflection, Time and the Novel: Toward a Communicative Theory of Literature*, London and Boston: Routledge and Kegan Paul.

Merleau-Ponty, Maurice (1962) *Phenomenology of Perception*, trans. Colin Smith, London and New York: Routledge.

Miller, J. Hillis (2001) *Others*, Princeton, NJ, and Oxford: Princeton University Press.

Morrison, Jago (2003) *Contemporary Fiction*, London and New York: Routledge.

Nietzsche, Friedrich (1968) *The Will to Power*, trans. Walter Kaufmann and R. J. Hollingdale. New York: Vintage.

Novikov, Igor (1998) *The River of Time*, trans. Vitaly Kisin, Cambridge: Cambridge University Press.

Popper, Karl (2002) *The Logic of Scientific Discovery*, London and New York: Routledge.

Prince, Gerald (1982) *Narratology*, Berlin, New York and Amsterdam: Monton.

Proust, Marcel (2003) *In Search of Lost Time*, trans. Lydia Davis, Harmondsworth: Penguin.

Punday, Daniel (2003) *Narrative after Deconstruction*, Albany, NY: State University of New York Press.

Ricoeur, Paul (1984) *Time and Narrative*, Vol. 1, trans. Kathleen McLaughlin and David Pellauer, Chicago: University of Chicago Press.

Ricoeur, Paul (1985) *Time and Narrative*, Vol. 2, trans. Kathleen Blamey and David Pellauer, Chicago: University of Chicago Press.

Ricoeur, Paul (1988) *Time and Narrative*, Vol. 3, trans. Kathleen Blamey and David Pellauer, Chicago: University of Chicago Press.

Ridderbos, K. (ed) (2002) *Time*, Cambridge: Cambridge University Press.

Rimmon-Kenan, Shlomith (1983) *Narrative Fiction: Contemporary Poetics*, London and New York: Methuen/Routledge.

Royle, Nicholas (2003) *The Uncanny*, Manchester: Manchester University Press.

Sartre, Jean-Paul (1969) *Being and Nothingness: An Essay on Phenomenological Ontology*, trans. Hazel E. Barnes, London and New York: Methuen/Routledge.

Simms, Karl (2003) *Paul Ricoeur*, London and New York: Routledge.

Smith, Ali (2005) *The Accidental*, London: Hamish Hamilton.

Solomon, Robert (1987) *From Hegel to Existentialism*, Oxford and New York: Oxford University Press.

Spark, Muriel (1974) *The Driver's Seat*, Harmondsworth: Penguin.

Staten, Henry (1985) *Wittgenstein and Derrida*, Oxford: Basil Blackwell.

Swift, Graham (2002) *Waterland*, London: Picador.

Todorov, Tzvetan (2000) 'The Typology of Detective Fiction', in Lodge, N., and Wood, D. (eds), *Modern Criticism and Theory: A Reader* (2nd edn), London and New York: Longman. First published in 1966.

Tomachevsky, Boris (1971) 'Thematics', in Lemon, Lee T., and Reis, Marion (eds), *Russian Formalist Criticism*, Cambridge, MA: MIT Press.

Vonnegut, Kurt (1991) *Slaughterhouse Five*, London: Vintage.

Waugh, Patricia (1984) *Metafiction: The Theory and Practice of Self-Conscious Fiction*, London and New York: Methuen.

Wood, David (2001) *The Deconstruction of Time* (2nd edn). Evanston, IL: Northwestern University Press. First published by Humanities Press (1989).

Wood, Michael (2005) *Literature and the Taste of Knowledge*, Cambridge: Cambridge University Press.

Žižek, Slavoj (1999) *The Ticklish Subject: The Absent Centre of Political Ontology*, London and New York: Verso.

Index